HUN
RM.

W9-CAV-188

# BEYOND GOOD AND EVIL

FRIEDRICH NIETZSCHE

# BEYOND GOOD AND EVIL

Translated and with an
Introduction by Marianne Cowan

A GATEWAY EDITION

HENRY REGNERY COMPANY

CHICAGO

Copyright 1955 by Henry Regnery
Company, Chicago, Illinois, Copyright
under International Copyright Union.
Manufactured in the United States of
America.

Eighth Printing 1969

# INTRODUCTION

Nietzsche has always been more popular with ordinary people than with professional philosophers and among ordinary people it has been chiefly the young who kept his memory alive. In 1944, when Nietzsche, on the occasion of the hundredth anniversary of his birth, was last mentioned in the more popular journals, the consensus of American opinion seemed to be that like his adversary Socrates, he was still the "seducer of youth." Necessary, perhaps, but to be hedged in with safeguards. Certainly he is still very much a weapon in the struggle of the young to individuate and distinguish themselves from the old. But the young need all the weapons they can learn to handle. It is to them that these notes are chiefly addressed.

*Beyond Good and Evil* is a book about morality. Nietzsche divides it into "articles" like articles of faith, but there is irony in this. For he says neither "thou shalt" nor "thou shalt not." Instead, he asks questions and he points out what it means to have lived with moral imperatives all one's life—not only one's own, but those of the human race. At the onset of the twentieth century Nietzsche sees humanity at the end of a long experiment with morality. We have defined and refined our ideas of good and evil so long, he says, that they are all worn out. They slip through our fingers and have a disconcerting way of turning into their opposites without notice. Turn over a good, like motherlove, and you find an evil: mother-domination, "smother-love." Squeeze an evil, like selfishness, and out slips a good: self-respect, self-control. Are we necessarily telling the truth when we are being "truthful"? What we do not wish to admit is that morality has been an experiment. We have come to a place where good and evil are no longer distinguishable to the naked eye. To distinguish them we must wear the colored glasses of some specific moral philosophy or habit. If such spectacles are a part of us, well and good. Nietzsche never wished to deprive anyone of his faith. On the contrary, as he says in this book, he would rather not be understood because of the enormous suffering that must be the base for understanding him. But if the wind of chance or a square right to the jaw has once knocked off the moral spectacles, what then? Once they are gone, we may not be able to get another pair.

Now at this point a great many people stop reading Nietzsche. At least they stop reading him intelligently. He lands one in nihilism, they say—both those who like being landed there and those who do not. But this is not true, however often it has been said. Nietzsche may have formulated more questions than answers, but even his questions are always suggestive. "Why don't we experiment with this and see where it leads us?" is the typical Nietzschean question. "Freedom of the will" is a good example that Nietzsche uses in this book. We have tried saying "My will is free to make any moral choice, such as that between right and wrong," and we have had to take our answer from biologists and psychologists and sociologists who point out how forces greater than ourselves manipulate us against our best, or worst, will. At intervals, however, and often simultaneously with the other, we have said, "Our will is not free" and have known immediately that this denies one of our greatest intuitive certainties: that we can now do *this* rather than *that,* that responsibility for oneself has some meaning. In many activities of life such fundamental oppositions are resolved for all practical purposes. When two opposite hypotheses meet head-on in science, for example, we can either wait for one to be better substantiated than the other, or we can drop the problem in that impossible formulation and perhaps solve it from another point of view entirely, when we are interested in something else. In morality we have felt that we could neither give in nor wait. "Why not?" asks Nietzsche. What binds us to absolutes in morality? Language, custom, our own unconscious intentions, our universal tendency to fear the unspeakable in ourselves and hence see it in others wherever we look. "Can this be helped?" asks Nietzsche further. "Must we give up morality when our present goods and evils fail us?" Here history helps us, and much of this book concerns itself with history. As we see in *perspective* (one of Nietzsche's favorite words) a long line of development in morality, we can begin to ask intelligent questions, and perhaps even start to give sensible answers, about the further history, the future development, of morality. In another book, *The Genealogy of Morals,* Nietzsche has outlined two simultaneously existing systems, that of "good vs. evil" and that of "good vs. bad." (There are several sections on them in this book, also.) But he does not mean that morality is exhausted in these two systems, even though from his point of view, he prefers one to the other. What he suggests here is quite the contrary, namely that it may be a good idea, right now, to give up the whole problem of "vs." with its mechanical dialectics.

The name of this book, for example, is *Jenseits*

*von Gut und Boese*. The word "beyond" with its
overtones of the "Great Beyond" gives some of the
flavor of the German *jenseits* but it does not exhaust
it. Fortunately Nietzsche expounds his meaning several times within the book. One meaning is "on the
other side of good and evil," indicating that good
and evil together are on the same side of morality
and that there exists another side. Another meaning
of *jenseits* is "aside from," i.e., paying no attention
to good and evil. When Nietzsche says that "What
is done out of love always happens beyond good
and evil," he places the full meaning of "beyond"
at our disposal—the "beyond" here is an "above"
and an "aside from" and a "without reference to."

So far the substance, the content, of Nietzsche's
book has been stressed. But the form of a book, too,
is a part of the content and this is as important in
Nietzsche as it is in James Joyce. Nietzsche's style
is colloquial and "difficult" by turns and often at
the same moment. It might be wise to start one's
reading with what he had to say about literary style
(sections 27, 28, 246, 247) to get a feeling for it,
and then to practice this feeling on the long first
sentence in section 295, in order to experience "lis-
tening with the third ear," to what Nietzsche calls
"tempo" and "nuance." Everywhere the book is full
of tricks. Nietzsche is famous, for example, for the
outrageous things he says about women. But in the
small section 231, which is easily and quite frequently
overlooked, he makes it evident that he never talks
more clearly and fundamentally about himself than
when he talks about "women as such." A typical
Nietzschean trick is to leave out the conclusion at
the end of a long chain of argument and to indicate
it with a dash or a series of dots. He once said in a

letter that everything he ever wrote came to life for him only after the final dash—everything before it was merely scenery. In section 194, for example, he only leads up to but never tells the point which is that a man does not "possess" anything until he is "possessed"—with the pun thrown in for good measure. In section 15 he not only fails to draw the conclusion expressly but with the very punctuation of the final sentence manages to throw the whole argument into a fascinating light of ambiguity.

There is a good deal of good-natured playfulness in this book. Take the chapter headings alone. The irony of calling them "Articles" has been mentioned. "The Free Thinker" is a sort of pun on "free-thinking." "Peoples and Fatherlands" has a tongue-in-cheek flavor in its plural of fatherland. The poem at the end of Article Eight is a magnificent parody of Wagner's peculiar literary style.

Nor are the "Prelude" of the subtitle, the "Entr'-acte" of aphorisms in the middle, and the "Postlude" in the form of a poem at the end just ornaments. They all give a clue to the dramatic, even musical quality that is Nietzsche's veritable signature as an artist. He did not mean that his philosophy should be a dull and overwhelming matter fit for the class room only. He practiced well the art of nuance of which he speaks, and the art of baiting with delicious tid-bits. He is truly a fisher of men; one who loves sailors and other fishermen, the imaginary audience of his books that he describes in *Thus Spoke Zarathustra*:

"To you alone, you bold seekers, tempters, experimenters, and to all who ever went out on the terrible sea with cunning sails—

To you alone, you who are riddle-drunk and twilight-happy, whose souls are lured by flutes to any treacherous chasm—

To you who do not like to grope for a clue with cowardly hands and who prefer not to deduce where you can intuit—

To you alone I shall tell the riddle that I saw. . . ."

MARIANNE COWAN

# PREFACE

Supposing that Truth is a woman—well, now, is there not some foundation for suspecting that all philosophers, insofar as they were dogmatists, have not known how to handle women? That the gruesome earnestness, the left-handed obtrusiveness, with which they have usually approached Truth have been unskilled and unseemly methods for prejudicing a woman (of all people!) in their favor? One thing is certain: she has not been so prejudiced. Today, every sort of dogmatism occupies a dismayed and discouraged position—if, indeed, it has maintained any position at all. For there are scoffers who maintain that dogma has collapsed, even worse, that it is laboring to draw its last breath. Seriously speaking, there are good grounds for hoping that all philosophic dogmatizing, however solemn, however final and ultimate it has pretended to be, may after all have been merely a noble child's-play and mere beginning. And perhaps the time is very near when we shall again and again comprehend *how* flimsy the cornerstone has been upon which the dogmatists have hitherto built their sublime and absolute philosophical edifices. Perhaps it was only some popular superstition of time immemorial (for example the soul-superstition which, in the guise of subject- and ego-superstition, has not ceased doing mischief even today); perhaps it was some play upon words, some seduction on the part of grammar, or some reckless generalization of very narrow, very personal, very human-all-too-human facts. The philosophy of the dogmatists, we hope, was only a promise held out over the millenniums, similar to astrology in still earlier times—astrology in whose service perhaps

more labor, more money, more sharp-wittedness and
patience have been spent than on any real science so
far. To astrology and its "ultra-mundane" claims in
Asia and Egypt we owe the grand style in architec-
ture. It seems that in order to inscribe themselves
upon the heart of humanity with everlasting claims,
all great things must first sweep the earth disguised
as enormous and fearsome grotesques. Dogmatic
philosophy has been such a grotesque—witness the
Vedanta doctrine in Asia and Platonism in Europe.
Let us not be ungrateful to it, although it must surely
be confessed that the worst, the most tiresome, and
the most dangerous of all errors hitherto has been a
dogmatist error: namely Plato's invention of Pure
Spirit and of the Good in Itself. But now that it has
been surmounted, now that Europe, rid of this nightmare, can again draw breath freely and at least enjoy
a healthier sleep, now *we, whose task it is to stay
awake,* we are the heirs of all the power gathered by
the fight against this error. To be sure, it meant turning the truth upside down, denying *perspectivity* (the
basic condition of all life), to speak of Spirit and of
the Good as Plato had spoken of them. Indeed, like
a physician one might ask, "How did such a disease
attack that finest product of antiquity, Plato? Did
that wicked Socrates really corrupt him after all?
Was Socrates after all the corrupter of youth and
deserving of his hemlock?" But the fight against
Plato, or—to speak plainer and for "the people"—
the fight against millenniums of Christian-ecclesiastical
pressure (for Christianity is Platonism for "the
people"), this fight created in Europe a magnificent
tension of spirit, such as had not existed anywhere
before. With such a tight-strung bow one can now
aim at the remotest targets. European man, to be

sure, feels this tension as a state of necessitation, and two attempts in grand style have been made to discharge the bow: once through Jesuitism and the second time through democratic enlightenment. This last attempt, in fact, aided by freedom of the press and the prevalence of newspaper-reading, might bring it to pass that Spirit will no longer so easily feel itself "necessary"! (The Germans invented gunpowder— all credit to them! But they made up for it by inventing the printing press.) We, however, who are neither Jesuits nor democrats nor even very German, we *good Europeans* and free, *very* free thinkers—we have it still, all the necessitation of spirit and all the tension of its bow! And perhaps also the arrow, the task, and (who knows?) the *target*. . . .

Sils-Maria, Upper Engadine. June, 1885.

# FIRST ARTICLE

## ABOUT PHILOSOPHERS' PREJUDICES

### 1.

The will to truth! That will which is yet to seduce us into many a venture, that famous truthfulness of which all philosophers up to this time have spoken reverently—think what questions this will to truth has posed for us! What strange, wicked, questionable questions! It has been a long story—and yet it seems hardly to have started. No wonder if just for once we become suspicious, and, losing our patience, impatiently turn around! Let us learn to ask this Sphinx some questions ourselves, for a change. Just *who* is it anyway who has been asking these questions? Just *what* is it in us that wants "to approach truth"? Indeed, we tarried a long time before the question of the cause of this will. And in the end we stopped altogether before the even more basic question. We asked "What is the value of this will?" Supposing we want truth: *why not rather* untruth? Uncertainty? Even Ignorance? The problem of the value of truth confronted us—or were we the ones who confronted the problem? Which of us is Oedipus? Which of us the Sphinx? It is a rendezvous of questions and question marks. It may be unbelievable, but it seems to us in the end as though the problem had never yet been posed—as though it were being seen, fixed, above all *risked,* for the first time. For there is a risk in posing it—perhaps no greater risk could be found.

## 2.

How is it possible for anything to come out of its opposite? Truth, for example, out of error? Or the will to truth out of the will to deception? Or a selfless act out of self-interest? Or the pure sunny contemplation of a wise man out of covetousness? This sort of origin is impossible. Who dreams of it is a fool or worse; the things of highest value must have some other, *indigenous* origin; they cannot be derived from this ephemeral, seductive, deceptive, inferior world, this labyrinth of delusion and greed! Their basis must lie in the womb of Being, in the Eternal, in the hidden God, in the "Thing In Itself" —here, and nowhere else!—This type of judgment is the typical prejudice by which the metaphysicians of all time can be recognized. This type of valuation stands back of all their logical methods; this is the "faith" that enables them to struggle for what they call "knowing"—a something which at last they solemnly christen "truth." The basic faith of all metaphysicians is *faith in the antithetical nature of values.* It has never occurred to the most cautious of them, even though they had taken the vow to "doubt everything," to pause in doubt at the very threshold where doubt would have been most necessary. But we may indeed doubt: first, whether antitheses exist at all, and second, whether those popular valuations and value-antitheses upon which the metaphysicians have placed their stamp of approval are not perhaps merely superficial valuations, merely provisional perspectives—and perspectives from a tight corner at that, possibly from below, a "worm's eye view" so to speak. Admitting all the value accorded to the true, the truthful, the selfless, it is nonetheless possible that a higher value should be ascribed to appearance, to the will to deception, to self-interest, to greed—a higher value with respect to all life. Furthermore, it is quite possible that the very value of those good and honored things consists, in fact, in their insidious relatedness to these wicked, seemingly opposite things—it could be that they are inextricably bound up, entwined, perhaps even similar in their very nature. Perhaps! But who is willing to be troubled by such a perilous Perhaps? We must wait for a new species of philosopher to arrive, who will have some other, opposite tastes and inclinations than the previous ones. Philosophers of the Perilous Perhaps, in every sense! And seriously, I can see such new philosophers coming up over the horizon.

### 3.

After keeping an eye on and reading between the lines of the philosophers for a long time, I find that I must tell myself the following: the largest part of conscious thinking must be considered an instinctual activity, even in the case of philosophical thinking. We must simply re-learn, as we have had to re-learn about heredity and "inborn" qualities. As little as the act of birth is of consequence in the whole process and progress of heredity, so little is consciousness in any decisive sense opposed to instinct. Most of the conscious thinking of a philosopher is secretly guided by his instincts and forced along certain lines. Even behind logic and its apparent sovereignty of development stand value judgments, or, to speak more plainly, physiological demands for preserving a certain type of life. Such as for example, that the definite is worth more than the indefinite, that appearance is less valuable than "the truth." Such valuations, all their regulative importance notwith-

*NOT AN INDEPENDANT THINKER*
*↳ GUIDED BY A LOGICAL SUPERSTRUCTURE*

standing, can for *us* be only foreground-valuations, a definite type of ridiculous simplicity, possibly necessary for the preservation of the creature we happen to be. Assuming, to be sure, that man does not happen to be "the measure of all things". . . .

### 4.

The falseness of a given judgment does not constitute an objection against it, so far as we are concerned. It is perhaps in this respect that our new language sounds strangest. The real question is how far a judgment furthers and maintains life, preserves a given type, possibly cultivates and trains a given type. We are, in fact, fundamentally inclined to maintain that the falsest judgments (to which belong the synthetic *a priori* judgments) are the most indispensable to us, that man cannot live without accepting the logical fictions as valid, without measuring reality against the purely invented world of the absolute, the immutable, without constantly falsifying the world by means of numeration. That getting along without false judgments would amount to getting along without life, negating life. To admit untruth as a necessary condition of life: this implies, to be sure, a perilous resistance against customary value-feelings. A philosophy that risks it nonetheless, if it did nothing else, would by this alone have taken its stand beyond good and evil.

### 5.

What tempts us to look at all philosophers half suspiciously and half mockingly is not so much that we recognize again and again how innocent they are, how often and how easily they make mistakes and

lose their way, in short their childishness and
childlike-ness—but rather that they are not sufficiently
candid, though they make a great virtuous noisy
to-do as soon as the problem of truthfulness is even
remotely touched upon. Every one of them pretends
that he has discovered and reached his opinions
through the self-development of cold, pure, divinely
untroubled dialectic (in distinction to the mystics of
every rank who, more honest and fatuous, talk about
"inspiration"), whereas, at bottom, a pre-conceived
dogma, a notion, an "institution," or mostly a heart's
desire, made abstract and refined, is defended by
them with arguments sought after the fact. They are
all of them lawyers (though wanting to be called
anything but that), and for the most part quite sly
defenders of their prejudices which they christen
"truths"—*very* far removed they are from the courageous conscience which admits precisely this; very
remote from the courageous good taste which makes
sure that others understand—perhaps to warn an
enemy or a friend, perhaps from sheer high spirits
and self-mockery. The spectacle of old Kant's Tartuffery, as stiff as it is respectable, luring us onto the
dialectical crooked paths which lead (or better, mis-
lead) to his "categorical imperative"—this spectacle
makes us, used to diversions as we are, smile. For
we find no small entertainment in keeping our eye
on the delicate tricks of ancient moralists and
morality-preachers. Or consider that hocus-pocus of
mathematical form with which Spinoza masked and
armor-plated as though in bronze his philosophy (or
let us translate the word properly: "the love of *his
own* wisdom")! He used it to intimidate at the very
start the courageous attacker who might dare cast

eyes on this invincible virgin and Pallas Athene—
how much insecurity and vulnerability this masquerade of a sick recluse betrays!

### 6.

Gradually I have come to realize what every great
philosophy up to now has been: the personal con-
fession of its originator, a type of involuntary and
unaware memoirs; also that the moral (or amoral)
intentions of each philosophy constitute the proto-
plasm from which each entire plant has grown. Indeed, one will do well (and wisely), if one wishes
to explain to himself how on earth the more remote metaphysical assertions of a philosopher ever
arose, to ask each time: What sort of morality is
this (is *he*) aiming at? Thus I do not believe that
a "desire for comprehension" is the father of philosophy, but rather that a quite different desire has here
as elsewhere used comprehension (together with
miscomprehension) as tools to serve its own ends.
Anyone who looks at the basic desires of man with
a view to finding out how well they have played
their part in precisely this field as inspirational genii
(or demons or hobgoblins) will note that they have
all philosophized at one time or another. Each individual desire wants badly to represent itself as *the*
final aim of existence and as rightful master of all
the others. For each desire is autocratic and *as such*
it attempts to philosophize. In the case of scholars,
to be sure, the specifically "scientific" men, it may
be different—"better" if you wish. They may really
have something like a "desire for comprehension,"
some small independent clockwork mechanism which,
when properly wound, works bravely on *without* in-

volving the remaining desires of the scholars. The
real "interests," therefore, of the scholars lie in
quite another field—in their family, perhaps, or their
livelihood, or in politics. It makes almost no difference, in fact, whether the little machine is em-
ployed in one place or another to serve science, and
whether the "promising" young worker makes of himself a philologist or a mushroom-fancier or a chemist
—his becoming this or that does not *characterize*
him. Conversely, there is nothing impersonal whatever in the philosopher. And particularly his morality
testifies decidedly and decisively as to *who he is*—
that is, what order of rank the innermost desires of
his nature occupy.

## 7.

How malicious philosophers can be! I know of
nothing more ferocious than the jest that Epicurus
permitted himself against Plato and the Platonists.
He called them *Dionysiokolakes*. Superficially, and
literally, it means "flatterers of Dionysius," that is
"yes-men" and lick-spittles; but in addition the word
signifies "They are only actors; they are not genuine"
(for Dionysiokolax was the popular designation for
an actor). This latter implication is really the malice
that Epicurus aimed at Plato; he was annoyed by the
grand manner, the play-acting, that Plato and all
his students so well knew how to put on—and
Epicurus did not! He, the old schoolmaster of Samos,
sat hidden in his little garden at Athens and wrote
three hundred books. Who knows—perhaps out of
furious ambition to equal Plato! It took one hundred
years before Greece realized just who this garden-god
Epicurus had been. If, indeed, she ever realized it!

### 8.

In every philosophy there comes the point where the philosopher's "conviction" enters the scene—or, in the words of an ancient mystery,

> *adventavit asinus*
> *pulcher et fortissimus.*[1]

### 9.

"In moderation, according to nature" you wish to live? Oh noble Stoics! How your words deceive! Think of a being like Nature, immoderately wasteful, immoderately indifferent, devoid of intentions and consideratenesses, devoid of compassion and a sense of justice, fruitful and desolate and uncertain at the same time; think of Indifference on the throne —how could you live in moderation according to this indifference? Living—isn't it precisely a wishing-to-be-different from this Nature? Doesn't living mean evaluating, preferring, being unjust, being limited, wanting to be different? But supposing your imperative "to live in moderation, according to nature" only means 'to live in moderation, according to life"— how then could you live *otherwise?* Why make a principle of something that you are and have to be? The truth is quite another matter: while rapturously pretending to read the canon of your law out of nature, you actually want the opposite—you strange play-actors and self-deceivers! Your pride wants to dictate your morality, your ideal, to nature (even to nature!). It wants to incorporate itself in nature; you demand that nature be nature "in moderation, ac-

[1] Entered now the ass _INSTINCT_
Beautiful and most strong.

cording to the Stoa"; you want to remake all existence to mirror your own existence; you want an enormous everlasting glorification of stoicism! With all your love for truth, you force yourselves to see nature *falsely,* i.e. stoically—so long, so insistently, so hypnotically petrified, until you can no longer see it any other way. And in the end some abysmal arrogance gives you the insane hope that, *because* you know how to tyrannize over yourselves (stoicism is self-tyranny), you can also tyrannize over nature—for isn't the Stoic a *part* of nature? . . . But all this is an old, everlasting story. What happened to the Stoics still happens today, as soon as a philosophy begins to have faith in itself. It always creates the world in its own image; it cannot do otherwise, for philosophy *is* this tyrannical desire; it is the most spiritual will to power, to "creation of the world," to the *causa prima.*

## 10.

The eagerness and artfulness (I should perhaps better say shrewdness) with which everyone in Europe today attacks the problems of "the real and the apparent world" gives us to think and to listen. Anyone who hears only a "will to truth" in the background surely does not enjoy the keenest hearing. In individual and rare cases there may really be involved such a will to truth—some extravagant and adventurous bravery, some metaphysician's ambition to deal with a lost cause. There may be a few who really prefer a handful of "certainty" to a whole wagonload of beautiful possibilities; there may even be some puritanical fanaticists of conscience who would prefer a certain nothing to an uncertain something—for a deathbed! But this is nihilism and the

token of a despairing soul, weary unto death, however brave the gestures of such a virtue may look.
But the stronger, livelier thinkers who are still thirsty
for life seem to feel otherwise. By taking sides
*against* appearance, by pronouncing the word "perspective" with arrogance, by valuing the authenticity
of their own bodies as highly as they value the evidence of their eyes which tells them that "the earth
stands still," by thus letting their surest possession
slip from their hands with apparent good humor (for
what do we believe in more firmly nowadays than
our own bodies?)—by doing all this—who knows?
—perhaps they really want to re-conquer old ground,
something that we used to possess with *greater certainty,* a something or other of the old domain of
our former faith, perhaps the "immortal soul," perhaps the "ancient God." In short, they would discover ideas upon which to build better, i. e. stronger
and more serene lives than one can build on "modern ideas." In these thinkers there is *suspicion*
against modern ideas; there is disbelief in everything
that was built yesterday and today; mixed up with
these there is perhaps some slight weariness and
scorn, some inability to stand the bric-a-brac of concepts of so many different origins, which so-called
positivism nowadays displays itself to be in the open
market place. A more refined taste feels nausea
when faced with the circus-poster crassness and
patchiness of all these reality-philosophasters who
have nothing new or genuine about them except this
crazy-quilt quality. We ought, it seems to me, agree
in this one particular with the skeptical anti-realists
and knowledge-microscopists of today; their instinct
which drives them away from *modern* reality is un-
refuted. And what do we care about their crooked

paths of regression! Their essential importance does *not* lie in the fact that they want to get "back" but that they want to get *away*. A little more energy, wingedness, courage, and craftsmanship—and they would want "out"—not back!

### 11.

It seems to me that everyone nowadays tries to divert attention from Kant's actual influence on German philosophy and wisely to gloss over the value which Kant himself ascribed to himself. Above everything else, Kant was proud of his table of categories. With this tablet in his hands, he proclaimed that "it is the most difficult task that ever could have been undertaken in the service of metaphysics." Let us understand rightly his "could have been"! He was proud of having *discovered* a new faculty in man—the faculty of making synthetic *a priori* judgments. Agreed that he deceived himself, nonetheless the development and rapid efflorescence of German philosophy depends on this pride. It is the ambition and rivalry of all the younger philosophers to discover something even more proud, if possible—and in any case to discover "new faculties"! But let us take thought: the time for it has come. How are synthetic *a priori* judgments *possible,* Kant asked himself. And what was actually his answer? *By virtue of a virtue*—but unfortunately not in five words but so complicatedly, respectably, with such a show of German profundity and sinuosity, that one failed to hear the funny German simple-mindedness inherent in such an answer. In fact we were beside ourselves about this new virtue and our joy reached its peak when Kant in addition discovered a moral virtue in man. For at that time the Germans were still moral and not a bit "politically realistic"! Now came the honeymoon of German philosophy. All the young theologians of the *Tübinger Stift* went beating the bushes for "virtues." And what all didn't they find—in that innocent, abundant, still youthful period of the German spirit, when Romanticism, the wicked fairy godmother, was still piping and singing; in those bygone days when "discovering" and "inventing" were still thought of as interchangeable! Above all, a virtue for the "transcendental." Schelling christened it "intellectual intuition," thereby anticipating the dearest heart's desire of his basically pious-minded Germans. One can do no worse injustice to this whole high-spirited and enthusiastic movement (which was youth, however much it disguised itself with gray and hoary concepts) than to take it seriously or—even worse—to treat it with moral indignation. Enough: they got older: the dream vanished. There came a time when they rubbed their eyes. We are still rubbing them today. It had been a dream; first and foremost a dream of old Kant's. "By virtue of a virtue," he had said, or at least meant. But is that—an answer? An explanation? Isn't it merely begging the question? How does opium induce sleep? "By virtue of a virtue"—the *virtus dormitiva,* says that physician in Molière:

> *quia est in eo virtus dormitiva,*
> *cujas est natura sensus assoupire*[2]

But this kind of answer belongs to comedy. It is finally time to replace the Kantian question, "How are synthetic *a priori* judgments possible?" with another question: "Why is it *necessary* to believe in

[2] Because there is in it a soporific virtue
The nature of which is to numb the senses

such judgments?" It is time for us to comprehend
that such judgments must be *believed* true (false as
they may actually be!) in order to preserve creatures
such as we are. Or, to say it more plainly, rudely,
and forthrightly: Synthetic *a priori* judgments should
not "be possible" at all; we have no right to them;
coming from us they are all false judgments. Only
it must not be forgotten that faith in their truth is
necessary; necessary as a provisional faith, an "eye-
witness faith," that has its place in the perspectivity-
optics of life. In order to say a final word about the
enormous influence that "German philosophy" (the
use of quotation marks will be understood, I trust)[3]
has had on all Europe: let there be no doubt that a
certain *virtus dormitiva* played its role. People were
in raptures because, thanks to German philosophy,
an antidote against the yet omnipotent sensualism
that they inherited from the previous century had
been found. It was found—among noble idlers, virtuous men, mystics, artists, three-quarter Christians,
and political obscurantists of all nations—in short,
*sensus assoupire*. . . .

## 12.

About materialistic atomism: it belongs among the
best refuted things that exist. Perhaps no one among
the scholars of Europe today is still so unscholarly
as to attach serious significance to it (other than
employing it as a handy abbreviation of means of
expression), thanks mainly to the Dalmatian, Boscovich, who, together with the Pole Copernicus, has
turned out to be the greatest and most successful op-

---

[3] The German expression for quotation marks is "little
goosefeet." *Tr.*

ponent of "eye-witness" evidence. Whereas Copernicus persuaded us to believe, contrary to the evidence
of all our senses, that the earth is *not* standing still,
Boscovich taught us to disavow our belief in the last
thing which remained "fast" on earth—namely our
faith in "substance," in "matter," in the final residue
of the universe, the little clod of atom. It was the
greatest triumph over the senses that has ever been
achieved on earth. But we must go further and declare war even on the "need for atomism," which
still leads a dangerous after-life in fields where no
one suspects its existence. We must next declare
relentless war onto death, as we did with that better
known "need for metaphysics," on that other and
more fateful atomism which Christianity has best and
longest taught: *psychic atomism*. With this expression let me designate the belief that the soul is something indestructible, eternal, non-divisible; that it is
a monad, an *atomon*. *This* faith ought to be eradi-
cated from science. Between ourselves, it will by
no means be necessary to get rid of the "soul" itself
in this process, and thereby do without one of the
oldest and most honorable hypotheses. This often
happens to unskilled naturalists: as soon as they
touch the "soul," they lose it. But we want the way
open to new formulations and refinements of the
soul-hypothesis. Concepts like "mortal soul" and
"the psyche as a manifold of subjectivity" and "the
psyche as social structure of the impulses and the
emotions" want henceforth to be admitted to scientific legitimacy. By putting an end to the supersti-
tions hitherto almost tropically rampant around the
ideas of soul, the *new* psychologist has pushed himself out, as it were, into new barrenness and new
suspicions. It may be that the older psychologists

had a jollier and more comfortable time—but in the end the new psychologist has sentenced himself to new inventions—and who knows?—perhaps new discoveries!

### 13.

The physiologists should take heed before they assume self-preservation as the cardinal drive of an organic being. Above all, a living thing wants to *discharge* its energy: life as such is will to power. Self-preservation is only one of its indirect and most frequent *consequences*. In short, here as elsewhere, beware of superfluous teleological principles, such as the instinct for self-preservation. (We owe it to Spinoza's inconsistency.) This is the first demand of methodology, which must in its essence be economy of principles.

### 14.

Today it is dawning on perhaps five or six minds that physics, too, is only an interpretation of the universe, an arrangement of it (to suit us, if I may be so bold!), rather than a clarification. Insofar as it builds on faith in sense-evidence, however, it is and shall long be taken for more—namely for a clarification. Physics has our eyes and fingers in its favor; it has eye-witness evidence and handiness on its side. This has an enchanting, persuasive, and *convincing* effect on any era with basically plebeian tastes; why, it follows instinctively the canon of truth of forever-popular sensualism. What is clear? What is "clarified"? Only that which can be seen and touched—to this extent must each problem be pursued. Conversely, the magic of Platonic thinking, a *distin-*

*guished* type of thinking, lay precisely in *resisting* obvious sense-evidence. This was the thinking of men who perhaps enjoyed stronger and more demanding senses than our contemporaries. But they knew how to find a greater triumph in remaining master of these senses, and they accomplished their aim by casting pale, cold, gray concept-nets over the motley sense-turmoil, the "pandemic" as Plato put it. There was an *enjoyment* in this kind of world-conquest and world-interpretation in the manner of Plato, quite different from that which the physicists of today offer us. And not only the physicists but the Darwinists and anti-teleologists among the physiological workers, with their principle of the "least possible effort" and the greatest possible stupidity. "Where there is nothing for man to see and grasp, man has no business to look"! That, to be sure, is an imperative quite different from the Platonic one. Yet, for a rough, industrious race of machinists and engineers of the future, who have nothing but rough work to do, it may just be the correct imperative.

### 15.

In order to work in the field of physiology with a clear conscience, one must insist that the sense organs are *not* phenomena in the idealist's sense— for if they were, they could not be causes! Thus we need sensualism at least as a regulative hypothesis if not as a heuristic principle. What? Others even say that the external world is the creation of our sense organs? But then our body, which is a part of the external world, would be the creation of our sense organs! But then our sense organs would be the creation of—our sense organs! This seems to me to be a thoroughgoing *reductio ad absurdum*, assuming that the concept *causa sui* is something thoroughly absurd. It follows, does it, that the external world is *not* the creation of our sense organs? . . .

## 16.

Even today there are still harmless self-observers who believe in "immediate certainties," such as, for example, "I think" or, in the formulation of Schopenhauer's superstition, "I will." They believe that cognition here gets hold of its object, naked and pure, as "thing in itself," and that there is no falsification, either by the subject or by the object. But I shall repeat a hundred times that "immediate certainty" as well as "absolute knowledge" and "thing in itself" are all contradictions in terms. Let us finally free ourselves of the seduction inherent in our vocabulary! Let the people believe that cognition has to do with simple recognition; the philosopher must say to himself something like this: when I analyze the process which is expressed in the sentence "I think," then I get a series of bold assertions whose proof would be difficult, perhaps impossible. For example, that it is *I* who do the thinking; that, more generally, there is a something which performs thinking; that thinking is an activity and an effect of a creature which is thought of as its cause; that there exists an "I"; finally, that it is already determined what is to be designated with the word "think," in other words, that I *know* what thinking is. For if I hadn't already decided what it was, how should I be able to distinguish what is happening now from what happens when I "will" or "feel"? Enough—the "I think" assumes that I *compare* my present condition with other conditions that I know

in myself, in order to determine what it is. Because
of this referral to other knowledge, "I think" for
me at least cannot have "immediate certainty."—In
place of that "immediate certainty," in which we
shall have to let the people believe in certain given
cases, the philosopher, as we see, gets his hands on
a series of metaphysical questions. They are real
intellectual questions of conscience: "Where do I
get the concept 'thinking'? Why do I believe in cause
and effect? What justifies me in speaking of an 'I,'
further, an 'I' which is a cause, further, an 'I' which
is a thought-cause?" Whoever dares make an immediate answer to such metaphysical questions,
basing his certainty on a sort of *intuition* of cognition (like the man who says "I think and know that
this at least is true, real, certain")—will get a smile
and two question marks from a philosopher nowadays. "My dear sir," the philosopher will most likely
give him to understand, "it is in truth unlikely that
you are not in error—but why must we have truth
at all cost, anyway?"—

## 17.

So far as the superstitiousness of logicians is concerned, I do not tire of emphasizing again and again
one little briefly stated fact which these superstitious
ones do not like to admit. It is simply this: A thought
comes when "it" will and not when "I" will. It is
thus a *falsification* of the evidence to say that the
subject "I" conditions the predicate "think." *It* is
thought, to be sure, but that this "it" should be that
old famous "I" is, to put it mildly, only a supposition, an assertion. Above all it is not an "immediate
certainty." In the end even "it is thought" says too
much. Even this "it" contains an *interpretation* of

the process and does not belong to the process itself. Our conclusion is here formulated out of our grammatical custom: "Thinking is an activity; every activity presumes something which is active, hence. . . ." According to this same approximate scheme, our older "astomism" was looking for the "force" that has an effect, for that little clod of matter that it inhabits, from which it acts; in short, the atom. More rigorous minds finally learned to get along without such "earthly remains," and perhaps in logic too we will some day become accustomed to getting along without that little "it" (into which the good old honest "I" has evaporated).

### 18.

It is surely not the smallest charm of a theory that it is refutable: this precisely attracts the subtler minds. It seems that the theory of "freedom of the will," a hundred times refuted, owes its permanence to just this charm. Someone always comes along who feels strong enough to refute it once more.

### 19.

Philosophers are in the habit of speaking of "will" as though it were the best-known thing in the world. Schopenhauer in fact gave us to understand that will alone is really known to us, completely known, known without deduction or addition. But it seems to me once again that Schopenhauer in this case too did only what philosophers are always doing: he took over and exaggerated a *popular judgment*. Willing seems to me to be, above all, something *complicated*, something that is a unity in word only. The popular judgment lies just in this word "only," and it has become master of the forever incautious phi-

losophers. Let us be more cautious, then; let us be
"unphilosophical"; let us say: in every willing there
is first of all a multiplicity of feelings: the feeling of
a condition to get *away* from, the feeling of a condition to get *to;* then the feeling of this "away" and
"to"; furthermore, an accompanying muscular feeling
which, from a sort of habit, begins a game of its own
as soon as we "will"—even without our moving our
"arms and legs." In the first place, then, feeling—
many kinds of feeling—is to be recognized as an
ingredient in willing. Secondly, there is thinking:
in every act of the will there is a thought which gives
commands—and we must not imagine that we can
separate this thought out of "willing" and still have
something like will left! Thirdly, the will is not
merely a complex of feeling and thinking but above
all it is a passion—the passion of commanding. What
is called "freedom of the will" is essentially a passionate superiority toward a someone who must
obey. "I am free; 'he' must obey"—the consciousness of this is the very willing; likewise that tension
of alertness, that straightforward look which fixes
on one thing exclusively, that absolute valuation
which means "just now this, and nothing else, is
necessary," that inner certainty that there will be
obedience—all this and whatever else is part of the
condition of one who is in command. A man who
*wills* is giving a command to something in himself
that obeys, or which he believes will obey. But now
let us note the oddest thing about the will, this manifold something for which the people have only one
word: because we, in a given case, are simultaneously
the commanders *and* the obeyers and, as obeyers,
know the feelings of forcing, crowding, pressing, resisting, and moving which begin immediately after

the act of the will: because, on the other hand, we are in the habit of glossing over this duality with the help of the synthetic concept "I"—for these reasons a whole chain of erroneous conclusions, and consequently false valuations of the will, has weighted down our notion of willing, so much so that the willer believes in good faith that willing *suffices* to produce action. Because in the majority of cases there was a willing only where the effect of the command, the obedience, i. e. the action, was an *expected* one, the *appearance* translated itself into the feeling that there had been a *necessary effect*. In short, the willer believes, with a considerable degree of certainty, that will and action are somehow one. He credits the success, the execution of the willing, to the will itself, therewith luxuriating in an increase of the feeling of power which all success produces. "Freedom of the will" is the word for that manifold pleasurable condition of the willer who is in command and at the same time considers himself as one with the executor of the command—as such enjoying the triumph over the resistance, but possessed of the judgment that it is his will itself that is overcoming the resistance. In this fashion the willer adds the pleasurable feelings of the executing, successful instruments, the subservient "lower wills" or "lower souls" (for our body is nothing but a social structure of many souls) to his pleasurable feeling as Commander. *L'effet c'est moi*—the same thing happens here that happens in any well constructed and happy community: the ruling class identifies itself with the success of the community. In all willing, then, there is commanding and obeying on the basis, as we have seen, of a social structure of many "souls." This is why a philosopher should consider himself justified in including willing within the general sphere of morality—morality understood as the doctrine of the rank-relations that produce the phenomenon we call "life."—

## 20.

The various philosophical concepts do not evolve at random or autonomously but in reference and relationship to one another; although they seem to occur suddenly and arbitrarily in the history of thought, they belong to a system exactly like all the members of the fauna of a continent. This is revealed by the fact that the most diverse philosophers again and again fill in a basic scheme of *possible* philosophies. Invisibly compelled, they revolve again and again in the same orbit. No matter how independent of each other they feel with their critical or systematic will—something or other in them leads them; something or other keeps them running, one after another, in a definite sequence. They share an inborn systematization and relation of concepts. Their thinking is in fact not so much a discovering as a recognizing, remembering, a return and a homecoming to a remote, ancient, commonly stocked household of the soul out of which the concepts grew. Seen in this light, philosophizing is a sort of atavism of the highest order. The odd family resemblance between all Indic, Greek, and German philosophizing is simple enough to explain. For especially where the languages are related it cannot possibly be avoided that, thanks to a common philosophy of grammar (by this I mean thanks to the unconscious domination and leadership of similar grammatical functions), everything lies prepared for a similar development and sequence of the various philosophical systems. For the same ɪeason, the road seems closed to certain other possibilities of word-interpretation. Philosophers belonging to the Ural-Altaic linguistic group (containing languages in which the concept of "subject" is least developed) most probably "view the world" quite differently and will be found on paths other than those travelled by speakers of Indo-European or by Moslems. The compulsion exerted by certain grammatical functions is in the end the compulsion of *physiological* value judgments and of the conditions that determine race.—This much by way of rejecting Locke's superficiality on the subject of the origin of ideas.

## 21.

The *causa sui* is the best self-contradiction hitherto thought up; it is a sort of logical rape and perversion. But man's extravagant pride has managed to tie itself up deeply and dreadfully with just this nonsense. The demand for "freedom of the will," in that metaphysical superlative sense in which it still rules the minds of the half-learned, the demand to assume the total and final responsibility for one's own actions, thereby relieving God, world, ancestors, accident, and society; this demand is nothing less than to be the *causa sui* oneself, to pull oneself by one's own bootstraps into existence out of the bog of non-existence—a feat dreamed up with a recklessness exceeding that of Baron Munchhausen! But supposing someone recognizes the peasant-like simplicity of our famous "freedom of the will" and deletes it from his thinking. I would now beg him to carry his "enlightenment" one step farther and to delete also contrary of that "free will" monstrosity. I mean the "non-free will," which amounts to a misuse of cause and effect. One should not mistakenly *objectivize* "cause" and "effect" in the manner of the natural scientists (and whoever else nowadays naturalizes in his thinking), in accordance with the ruling mechanistic oafishness that pushes and pulls the cause until it becomes "effective." One should make use of "cause" and "effect" only as pure *concepts,* i. e. as conventional fictions for the purpose of designation and mutual understanding, *not* for explanation. In "being-as-such" there are no "causal connections" or "necessities" or "psychological lack of freedom"; effect there does *not* follow upon a cause; there *is* no "law" which rules phenomena. It is *we,* we alone, who have dreamed up the causes, the one-thing-after-anothers, the one-thing-reciprocating-anothers, the relativity, the constraint, the numbers, the laws, the freedom, the "reason why," the purpose. And when we mix up this world of symbols with the world of things as though the symbols existed "in themselves," then we are merely doing once more what we have always done: we are creating myths. The "non-free will" is a piece of mythology; in real life there is only *strong* will and *weak* will. It is almost always a symptom of what the man lacks when a thinker feels something of constraint, necessity, having-to-obey, pressure, and lack of freedom in all his "causal connections" and "psychological necessities." It is revealing to feel these things: the personality betrays itself. On the whole, if I have observed correctly, there are two diametrically opposed factions which have picked the "non-freedom" of the will for their problem—but both sides reveal a profoundly *personal* bias. The ones want to avoid giving up at any cost their "responsibility," their faith in *themselves,* their personal right to *their* merit. (These are the vain races!) The others, conversely, do not want to be responsible for anything; they do not want to be guilty of anything; they demand, from an inner self-contempt, to *get rid of the burden* of themselves in some direction or other. When this latter type writes books, nowadays, they usually interest themselves in criminals: a sort of socialistic compassion is their favorite disguise. And they are right: the fatalism of the weak of will is astonishingly beautified by its claim to be *"la religion de la souffrance humaine."* Herein lies its type of "good taste."

### 22.

One will forgive, I hope, an old philologist who cannot desist from the malice of pointing his finger at poor interpretation. But really, that "conformity of nature unto law" of which you physicists talk so proudly as if . . . , that lawfulness is the result only of your *explication de texte,* of your bad philology! It is not a fact, not a "text" at all, but only a naive, humanitarian arrangement and misinterpretation that you use for truckling to the democratic instincts of the modern soul. "Everywhere equality before the law—and nature is no better off than we are"— surely a fine *arrière-pensée* in which are disguised first, a vulgar hostility to everything privileged and autocratic, and second, a very subtle atheism. *"Ni dieu, ni maitre"*—you, too, want that, and therefore "Long live natural law"! Am I right? But, as I have said , this is explication, not text, and someone might come along who, with opposite intention and inter-pretive skill, might read out of the same nature and the same phenomena quite another thing: a tyran-nical, inconsiderate, relentless enforcement of claims to power. There may arise an interpreter who might so focus your eyes on the unexceptionality and unconditionality of all "will to power" that almost every word that you now know, including the word "tyranny" would finally become useless and sound like a weakening and palliative metaphor—as something too human. And yet he might end by asserting about this world exactly what you assert, namely that it runs a "necessary" and "calculable" course—but *not* because it is ruled by laws but because laws are absolutely lacking, because at each moment each power is ultimately self-consistent. Let us admit that this, too, would be only an interpretation—and you will be eager enough to make this objection! Well, all the better!

### 23.

All psychology hitherto has become stuck in moral prejudices and fears: none has ventured into the depths. To consider psychology as the morphology and evolutionary doctrine of the will to power—as I consider it—this no one has touched upon even in thought (insofar as it is allowable to recognize in what has been written the symptoms of what has been kept dark). The force of moral prejudices has penetrated deeply into the most spiritual, the seemingly coldest and most open-minded world, and, as one may imagine, with harmful, obstructionist, blinding, and distorting results. A proper physio-psychology must battle with unconscious resistances in the heart of the investigator; his "heart" sides against it. Even a doctrine of the reciprocally limiting interaction of the "good" and "wicked" impulses causes, as being a subtle form of immorality, some distress and aversion in a still strong and hearty conscience. Even worse is a doctrine that all the good impulses are derived from the wicked ones. But imagine someone who takes the very passions—hatred, envy, greed, domineering—to be the passions upon which life is conditioned, as things which must be present in the total household of life. Takes them to be necessary in order to preserve the very nature of life, to be further developed if life is to be further developed! Such a man suffers from the inclination of his judgment as though from seasickness! But even this hypothesis is by no means the most painful or the strangest in this enormous, almost totally unknown domain of dangerous insights. Indeed, there are a hundred good reasons for staying away from it if one—can! On the other hand, if our ship has once taken us there—very well, let us go ahead, grit our teeth, open our eyes, grip the rudder and—ride out morality! Perhaps we will crush and destroy our own remaining morality, but what do *we* matter! Never yet has a *deeper* world of insight been opened to bold travellers and adventurers. And the psychologist who can make this sort of "sacrifice" (it is not the *sacrifizio dell' intelletto*—on the contrary!) will at least be in a position to demand that psychology be acknowledged once more as the mistress of the sciences, for whose service and preparation the other sciences exist. For psychology is now again the road to the basic problems.

# SECOND ARTICLE

## THE FREE THINKER

### 24.

*O sancta simplicitas!* How strangely simplified
and falsified does man live! One does not cease
to wonder, once one has eyes to see this wonder!
How bright and free and easy and simple we have
made everything around us! How well we knew
to give our senses a free ticket to everything superficial! How we have given our thinking a divine
yen for exuberant jumps and faulty conclusions!
How from the very beginning we have managed to
preserve our ignorance in order to enjoy a scarcely
comprehensible freedom, impetuosity, carelessness,
heartiness, and gaiety of life, in short—life! And
science up to now was allowed to rise only on this
firm, granite rock of ignorance; the will to know on
the foundation of a much more forceful will, namely
the will to not-know, to un-certainty, to un-truth!
Not as its opposite—no, as its refinement! Let
*language,* here as elsewhere, retain its awkwardness
and continue to talk about antitheses where there are
only degrees and diverse subtle levels; let the in-
veterate Tartuffery of morality which has become
our invincible flesh and blood twist even the words
of us knowing ones around in our mouths: never-
theless! Here and there we comprehend (and can
laugh about it) that the very best of science wants
to hold us fast to this *over-simplified,* thoroughly
artificial, made-over and falsified world. Why? Because science loves error, involuntarily-willingly; because science, alive, loves—life!

28

## 25.

After such a cheerful beginning, a serious word would like to be heard: it is directed to the most serious people. Beware, you philosophers and friends of insight, beware of martyrdom! Beware of suffering "in the cause of truth." Even of self-defense! It will spoil the innocence and the fine neutrality of your conscience; it will make you stubborn against objections and red rags, it stupefies, bestializes, and brutalizes you, if the battle with danger, slander, suspicion, exile, and even rougher consequences of hostility makes you act out the role of defender of the truth on earth! As though "the truth" were so harmless and maladroit a creature that it needed defenders,—needed you of all people, you knights of the most sorrowful countenance, my dear loafers and cobweb-spinners of the spirit! In the end you know well enough that it must not matter in the least whether or not *you* turn out to have been right. Furthermore, you know that no philosopher hitherto has ever turned out to have been right; that a more praiseworthy truthfulness lies in any little question mark that you conceal behind your favorite terms and doctrines (and occasionally behind yourselves) than in all your solemn gesturings and posturings in front of public accusers and halls of justice! Why don't you step aside, instead? Flee into concealment! And don your mask and your subtlety, so that you can be mistaken for someone else! Or feared a little! And don't forget the garden, the garden with the golden fence. And have people around you that are like a garden, or like music across still waters, at evening time when day turns into memory. Choose the *good* solitude, the free, playful, easy solitude that somehow gives you the right to remain good in some sense! How venomous, how crafty, how bad you grow in any long war which cannot be waged in open violence. How *personal* you grow through a long-lasting fear, a long-lasting look-out for enemies, possible enemies! These exiles from society, these long-persecuted, frightfully driven ones—also the hermits of necessity, the Spinozas or Giordano Brunos—in the end they always become subtly vengeful, and poison mongers (beneath even the most spiritual masquerade and possibly without realizing it themselves—just try digging up the grounds of Spinoza's ethics and theology!). Not to mention the foolishness of moral indignation which is the unmistakable sign in a philosopher that his philosophic sense of humor has left him. Martyrdom in a philosopher, his "self-sacrifice in the cause of truth," forces to the light whatever of play-actor and agitator is in him. Admitted that thus we have watched such people with mere esthetic curiosity, we can nonetheless comprehend the dangerous desire to see them exposed for once in their degenerate form (degenerated into "martyrs," i. e. stage and public tribunal "hams"). Only we must keep in mind *what* we shall see if we give in to such a desire—namely a satyr-play, a farcial postlude that is nothing but the continued proof that the long, actual tragedy is *at an end,* assuming that the development of any philosophy is one long tragedy.—

## 26.

Every select man seeks instinctively to find his castle, his secret place, where he is *absolved* of the mass, the many, the majority—where he may forget the human rule, being himself the exception. Unless one thing happens: unless by a still stronger instinct he is confronted directly by the rule. But then he has insight in the great and exceptional sense. Whoever does not occasionally glitter with all the colors of distress when confronted with human intercourse, whoever doesn't turn green and grey with nausea, surfeit, compassion, depression, and loneliness, is surely not a man of discriminating taste. But if he does not voluntarily assume all this burden and displeasure, if he constantly avoids it, remaining quietly and proudly hidden in his castle—well, one thing is then certain: he was not made, not predestined, for insight. If he were, he would have to tell himself one day, "Let the devil take my good taste—but the rule is more interesting than the exception, than I, the exception!" And he would come down; above all, he would "jump in." The study of the *average* man: long, earnest study, requiring much disguise, self-mastery, familiarity, and bad company (for every company except that of one's peers is bad company): this study makes up a necessary part of a philosopher's life history. Perhaps the most unpleasant, ill-smelling, disappointing part. But if he is lucky (as befits a love-child of insight), he will meet those who will substantially abbreviate and lighten his task. I mean the so-called cynics, those who simply acknowledge the beast, the vulgarity, the "rule" in themselves, and who have, in addition, the degree of intellectuality and wit necessary to discuss themselves and their like *in front of witnesses.* Occasionally they even wallow in books, as though in their own excrement. Cynicism is the only way in which vulgar souls can come close to candor, and the superior man has to open his ears

every time he hears a piece of coarse as well as
subtle cynicism, and to congratulate himself each
time that the shameless clown or the scientific satyr
chooses him to confide in. There are even cases
where fascination is mixed with one's nausea, where
through nature's caprice a genius is tied up with
some indiscreet goat or ape. The Abbé Galiani was
such a creature, the most profound, sharp-sighted
and possibly also filthiest man of his century—much
profounder than Voltaire and hence a good deal
more silent. A little more frequent an occurrence,
as I have indicated, is a scientific head on an ape's
body, or a fine, exceptional intelligence on a vulgar
soul. These are not a bit rare, especially among
physicians and morality-physiologists. Wherever
someone talks about man as a belly with two needs
and a head with one (and talks harmlessly, without
bitterness), wherever someone sees, seeks, and *wants*
to see only hunger, sex, and vanity as though they
were the genuine and only springs of human behavior, in short wherever they say "bad" (not even
"wicked") things about man—there let the expert
in insight listen with subtlety and diligence. In
general he should always have his ears open where
people talk without indignation. For the indignant
human being, the man who rends and lacerates himself with his own teeth (or, if not himself, then God,
world, or society as substitutes), may be morally
superior to the laughing and self-satisfied satyr, but
in every other respect he is the more ordinary, less
interesting, less instructive case. Besides no one *lies*
as much as an indignant man.—

27.

It is difficult to be understood, especially when one

thinks and lives *gangasrotogati* among people who
think and live quite otherwise, namely *kurmagati* or
at best *mandeikagati*—"the way a frog walks."
(You see, I do my best to be understood with difficulty.) One should be heartily grateful for at least
the intention to some degree of subtlety in interpretation. But so far as one's "good friends" are concerned, who are always too comfort-loving (and who
believe that this is the prerogative of friends), one
does well if one assigns to them at the very outset
some play and exercise room for misunderstanding.
Then one can at least laugh while one watches them.
Or one can get rid of these good friends altogether—
and then laugh!

### 28.

The hardest thing to translate from one language
to another is the tempo of its style. For it has its
foundations in the character of the race, or, more
physiologically, in the average rate of its "metabolism." There are honest, well-meant translations
which are almost falsifications, involuntary vulgariza-
tions of the original, just because the brave, jolly
tempo of the original could not be taken into account
—and it is this which helps the reader skip over the
dangers inherent in things and words. The German
is almost incapable of producing a *presto* in his
language; hence, we may justly deduce, incapable of
many of the most diverting and reckless nuances of
free-thinking thought. By as much as *buffo* and the
satyr are foreign to his body and his conscience, by
so much are Aristophanes and Petronius untranslat-
able for him. Everything grave, heavy-flowing, sol-
emn-pompous; all long drawn out and tiresome
species of style, are developed among Germans in

superabundant variety. Forgive me, but it is a fact
that even Goethe's prose in its mixture of stiffness
and fragility is no exception. It is a mirror of the
"good old days" to which it belongs—the days when
there was still a "German taste" and it was a rococo-
taste, in *moribus et artibus.* Lessing constitutes an
exception, thanks to his actor's nature that understood much and could handle many things. Not for
nothing was Lessing the translator of Bayle, and not
for nothing did he like to run away into the company
of Diderot and Voltaire and, even more, the Roman
comedy-writers. Even in tempo, Lessing loved free-
thinking, and that is to say, escape from Germany.
But how could the German language, even in the
prose of a Lessing, imitate the tempo of Machiavelli
who, in his *Principe,* lets us breathe the dry thin air
of Florence and who cannot resist presenting the
most serious matters in an ungovernable *allegrissimo*
—perhaps not without a malicious artist's inkling of
the antithesis he is venturing on: thoughts that are
long, difficult, hard, and dangerous—in a tempo of
galloping along in the best and most playful high
spirits. Who, finally, could venture a German trans-
lation of Petronius who was, more than any great
musician up to now, a master of *presto* in his inventions, notions, and words? What in the end do all
the swamps of the sick wicked world (even if it is
the "ancient world") matter if one has the feet of the
wind, like Petronius, and the draught and the breath
and the liberating mockery of the wind. Such a wind
cures everything because it makes everything *run.*
And as for Aristophanes, that transfiguring and com-
plementary spirit, for whose sake one *forgives* everything Greek for having existed (assuming one fully
comprehends *what* all needs forgiveness and required

transfiguration), I know of nothing which has made me day-dream more about *Plato's* concealed and sphinx-like nature than that happily preserved *petit fait:* under his pillow on his deathbed there was no "bible," no Egyptian, Pythagorean, or Platonic writings, but only a copy of Aristophanes. Of course! How could Plato have endured life (Greek life to which he said "no") without an Aristophanes!

### 29.

Very few people are capable of being independent; it is a privilege of the strong. And whoever tries it, however justified, without *having* to, proves that he is probably not only strong but bold to the point of complete recklessness. For he walks into a labyrinth; he increases a thousandfold the dangers which are inherent in life anyway. And not the smallest of his dangers is that no one can witness how and where he loses his way, falls into solitude, or is torn to pieces by some troglodytic minotaur of conscience. When such a man perishes, it happens so far from human understanding that other men have no feeling for it, no fellow feeling. But there is no return for him—not even a return to human compassion!—

### 30.

Our deepest insights must—and should—sound like follies and under certain circumstances like crimes when they come unauthorized to the ears of those who are not disposed toward and predestined for them. The exoteric and the esoteric types (as philosophers were formerly distinguished among Hindus, Greeks, Persians, Mussulmans, in short wherever people believed in gradations of rank and *not* in equality and equal rights)—these two types are not so much differentiated by the fact that the exoteric type stands without and views, evaluates, measures, and judges from without rather than from within, and that the converse is true of the esoteric type. The more essential distinction is that the exoteric type views things from below upwards, whereas the esoteric type views things *from above downwards*. There are heights of the soul from which even tragedy ceases to appear tragic. All the woe of the world taken together, who could dare decide whether the sight of it would *necessarily* seduce and constrain one to sympathy (in other words to a doubling of the woe)?—That which serves the higher type of man for nourishment or refreshment must be almost poison to an entirely distinct and lesser type of man. The virtues of the common man would perhaps amount to vices and weaknesses in a philosopher; it might be possible for a highly developed man, supposing he were to degenerate and go to ruin, in that very process to acquire qualities for whose sake he would have to be honored as a saint in the lower world into which he had sunk. There are books which have an inverse value for the soul and for health according to whether an inferior soul and lower vitality, or a higher and more powerful one, make use of them. In the first case they are dangerous books, contributing to decay and dissolution; in the second case they are heralds which summon the bravest to *their type* of bravery. Best-sellers are always ill-smellers, sticky with the odor of small people. Where the people eat and drink, and even where they worship, it usually stinks. One should not enter churches in order to find *fresh* air to breathe. . . .

When one is young one accords honor or con-

## 31.

tempt without that art of the nuance which constitutes the best profit to be had from life. And, as is quite just, one must do heavy penance for having attacked people and things with "yes" and "no," as it were. Everything is arranged in such a fashion that the worst of all tastes, the taste for the absolute, is cruelly teased and abused until finally man learns to incorporate some art into his feelings and to prefer, if necessary, to experiment with artificiality, like the real virtuosos of life. The anger and reverence that characterize youth seem not to rest until they can discharge themselves against them. The very essence of youth is falsification and deception. Then later, when the young soul, tortured by nothing but disappointments, finally turns on itself in suspicion (still hot and wild, even while suspicious and conscience-stricken)—how angry it is now at itself, how impatiently it rends itself, how it takes revenge for its long self-deception as though it had been a voluntary blindness! In this transition period one punishes oneself by mistrusting one's own feelings; one tortures one's enthusiasms by doubt; one goes so far as to consider one's good conscience a danger, one thinks of it as a self-obfuscation and a tiring of a more refined candor. But above all, one takes sides —basically and in principle—against "youth."—A decade later one comprehends that that stage too was—youth!

## 32.

For the longest period in human history (we call it the prehistoric period), the value or worthlessness of an action was inferred from its consequences. The action itself or the origin of the action was considered in the same light in which China even today considers the excellence or disgrace of a child—something which is a reflected quality of the parents. It was the reflecting force of success or failure which caused man to think well or ill of an action. Let us call this period of mankind the *pre-moral* period. The imperative "know thyself" was still unknown to it. In the last ten millenniums, on the other hand, we have progressed step by step in several large areas of the world to the point where we let not the consequences but the origins of an action determine its value. This, on the whole, was a momentous occurrence, a considerable refinement of our view and our criteria. It was the unconscious influence of the rule of aristocratic values, of belief in "descent"—tokens of a period which we may designate as *moral,* in the more narrow sense. It constitutes the first experiment in self-knowledge. Origin instead of consequences: what a reversal of perspective! A reversal surely arrived at only after long struggle and wavering! To be sure, it produced the rule of a new fateful superstition, a peculiar narrowness of interpretation. The origin of an action was interpreted to rest, in a very definite sense, on an *intent.* Everyone united in the one faith that the value of an action lay in the value of its intent. Intent as the sole origin and pre-history of an action: this is the prejudice that has dictated our moral praise, censure, judgments, and philosophy on earth till the most recent times.—But haven't we really arrived at the necessity today of once more resolving that there has been another reversal and basic shift of values, thanks to further self-recognition and self-deepening of man? Aren't

we standing on the threshold of a period which, pro-
visionally, we ought to label negatively as the *amoral*
period? At least among us immoralists today there
is arising a suspicion that the decisive value of an
action is precisely in what is *not* intentional in it;
that all its intentionality, everything that can be
seen, known, made conscious in it belongs only to
its surface, its skin which, like any skin, reveals
something but *conceals* even more! In short, we believe that intent is only a symbol and sympton, requiring interpretation; furthermore that it is a symbol
which signifies too much and consequently means
little if nothing by itself; that morality in the old
sense, i. e. morality of intent, was a prejudice, a
premature, perhaps a preliminary thing; something in
the order of astrology or alchemy, but in any event
something which must be surpassed. The surpassing
of morality, the self-surpassing of morality in a
certain sense: this may be taken to be the name
for that long secret labor which is in store for the
subtlest, most candid, also most malicious consciences of today. They are the living touchstones
of the soul!

### 33.

There is no help for it: we must mercilessly call
to account and bring to trial the feelings of surrender,
of self-sacrifice for one's fellow-man, all the morality
of self-alienation. And we must add to them the
esthetics of "disinterested perception" beneath which
the castrated art of today seeks seductively to create
a good conscience for itself. There is too much
charm and sugar in those feelings of "for others, *not*
for myself" for us not to feel the need of being

doubly suspicious and of asking whether they are
not by any chance *seductions!* For that they are
*pleasing* (to the one who has them, to the one whom
they benefit, and even to the mere spectator) is by
no means an argument *for* them. On the contrary,
it calls for caution. So let us be cautious!

### 34.

No matter from what philosophic point of vantage
one looks today, from any position at all, the *fal-
laciousness* of the world in which we think we live
is the firmest and most certain sight that meets our
eye. We find reason upon reason for this, and they
would lure us to surmise a deceptive principle in
"the nature of things." But whoever makes our
thinking, i. e. "mind," responsible for the world's
falseness (an honorable loophole through which
every conscious or unconscious *advocatus dei* slips),
whoever takes this world together with its space,
time, form and motion, to be falsely *inferred*, such
a man would have good reason to learn to distrust
all thinking altogether. For hasn't thinking, in such
a case, played the most incredible prank on us? And
who is to guarantee that it would not continue to do
what it has always done? In all seriousness, the innocence of thinkers has something touching about it.
It produces veritable reverence in us when we see
them, even today, stepping up to consciousness and
begging it to give them *honest* answers. "Are you
real?", they ask of consciousness, and "Why do you
keep the external world so resolutely away from
yourself?" and other such questions. Faith in "immediate certainties" is a *moral* naïveté that does
honor to us philosophers, but we were not made to
be *only moral* men. Aside from its morality, such

faith is a stupidity which does us little honor! Let middle-class society think of ever-ready mistrust as a sign of "bad character" and therefore count it among the imprudent qualities. Here, among us, beyond the middle classes and their "yes" and "no" —what should keep us from being imprudent and saying: the philosopher has a veritable *right* to have a "bad character." He is the creature who has heretofore been most easily fooled. Today he has the *duty* to be mistrustful, to squint most maliciously from every abyss of suspicion.—Forgive the jest of this gloomy caricature and turn of thought. But I myself have had to re-learn long ago; I have had to re-evaluate deceiving and being deceived; and I hold in readiness at least a couple of jabs in the ribs for the blind rage of philosophers who struggle against being deceived. Why *not?* It is no more than a moral prejudice that truth is worth more than semblance; in fact it is the worst-proved supposition that exists. Why don't we admit at least this much: there could be no life except on the basis of perspectival valuations and semblances. And if, with the virtuous enthusiasm and ineptitude of many philosophers, you wanted to get rid of the "world of semblance" altogether (assuming *you* could do this), well, there would be nothing left of your "truth," either. Whatever forces us, furthermore, to assume at all that there is an essential difference between "true" and "false"? Is it not sufficient to assume levels of semblance, lighter and darker shadows and tones of semblance as it were, different "values" in the painters' sense of the term? Why couldn't the world *which matters to us* be a fiction? And if someone asks, "But doesn't an originator go with a fiction?", couldn't he be answered roundly with "Why?" Couldn't this "go with" go with the fiction? Aren't we going to be allowed to be a little ironical about the subject, as much as about the predicate and the object? Isn't the philosopher allowed to raise himself above faith in grammar? All due respect to our schoolmarms, but isn't it time for philosophy to renounce the faith of schoolmarms?—

### 35.

O Voltaire! O humaneness! O idiocy! There is something about "truth," about the *search* for truth. If man goes about it too "humanely," it *"il ne cherche le vrai que pour faire le bien,"* [1] I bet he will find nothing.

### 36.

Let us assume that nothing is "given" as real except our world of desires and passions, that we cannot step down or step up to any kind of "reality" except the reality of our drives—for thinking is nothing but the interrelation and interaction of our drives. Would we not be allowed to experiment with the question whether these "givens" are not *sufficient* for understanding the so-called mechanistic (or material) world? I mean not as an illusion, "a semblance," an "idea" (in Berkeley's or Schopenhauer's sense), but as equal in reality-stature to our passions? To understand it as a more primitive form of the world of passions in which everything, still contained in a powerful unison, later branches off and develops (also, as is fair enough, weakens and is refined) in the organic processes? As a sort of primitive life in

---

[1] He seeks the truth only in order to do good.

which all the organic functions, together with self-regulation, assimilation, nutrition, secretion and metabolism, are still synthetically bound up with one another? To understand the material world as a *pre-form* of life? In the end this experimental question is not merely allowed; it is demanded by the conscience of *methodology*. Not to assume several types of causality until the experiment of getting along with a single one has been followed to its utmost conclusion (to the point of absurdity, if I may be permitted to say so): this is the morality of methodology which one may not escape today. It follows "from its definition" as a mathematician would say. In the end, the question is whether we really acknowledge the will as *effective;* whether we believe in the causality of the will. If we do (and basically our faith in the causality of the will amounts to our belief in causality itself), we *must* experiment with taking will-causality as our only hypothesis. Will, of course, can only act on will, not on matter (on "nerves," for example). Enough said: we must risk the hypothesis that everywhere we recognize "effects" there is an effect of will upon will; that all mechanical happenings, insofar as they are activated by some energy, are will-power, will-effects.—Assuming, finally, that we succeeded in explaining our entire instinctual life as the development and ramification of one basic form of will (of the will to power, as I hold); assuming that one could trace back all the organic functions to this will to power, including the solution of the problem of generation and nutrition (they are one problem)—if this were done, we should be justified in defining *all* effective energy unequivocally as *will to power*. The world seen from

within, the world designated and defined according to
its "intelligible character"—this world would be *will
to power* and nothing else.

### 37.

What did we say? Doesn't this mean, popularly
speaking, that God is refuted but the devil is not?
On the contrary, on the contrary, my friends. But
who the devil forces you to speak popularly, anyway?

### 38.

What happened during all the enlightenment of
recent times to the French Revolution may happen
again. Looked at closely, it was a gruesome farce,
and unnecessary; but from afar the noble and enthusiastic spectators of all Europe so passionately
read their own outrage and enthusiasm into it that
the text disappeared beneath the interpretation! So
a noble line of our descendants might misunderstand
us as we become the past, and thus make our sight
endurable after all. Or rather, hasn't this already
happened? Were we not ourselves this noble line of
descendants? And is it not all over—now that we
comprehend it?

### 39.

No one very easily takes a doctrine as true merely
because it makes one happy or virtuous. No one,
that is, but the lovely "idealists," who yearn over
the good, the true, and the beautiful and let every
kind of colorful, clumsy, and good-natured desir-
ability swim at random in their pool. Happiness and

virtue are not arguments. But we like to forget—
even sensible thinkers do—that things making for
unhappiness or for evil are not counter-arguments,
either. Something might be true, even though it is
harmful and dangerous in the greatest degree; it
might in fact belong to the basic make-up of things
that one should perish from its full recognition. Then
the strength of a given thinker would be measured
by the amount of "the truth" that he could stand.
Or, to say it more plainly, to what degree he would
*need* to have it adulterated, shrouded, seweetened,
dulled, and falsified. But there can be no doubt that
for the discovery of certain *parts* of the truth, evil
and unhappy men are better suited and have a
greater probability of obtaining success—not to
speak of those evil ones who are happy (a species
of man which the moralists keep dark). Perhaps
hardness and guile are better qualifications for the
development of a strong independent thinker and
philosopher than that gentle, delicate, yielding good
nature and skill for taking things lightly that we
value in an intellectual, and rightly so. Assuming
the obvious, that one does not narrow the concept
"philosopher" to the philosopher who writes books
or, worse yet, introduces his *own* philosophy into
books. A final feature of the freethinking philosopher is furnished by Stendhal whose words I shall
not omit to italicize for the sake of German taste—
for they run *counter* to German taste:

*"Pour être bon philosophe,"* says this last great
psychologist, *"il faut être sec, clair, sans illusion.
Un banquier, qui a fait fortune, a une partie du
charactère requis pour faire des découvertes en
philosophie, c'est-à-dire pour voir clair dans ce qui*

*est.*" (In order to be a good philosopher it is necessary to be dry, clear, without illusion. A banker who has made a fortune has one aspect of character needed to make discoveries in philosophy: that is to say, he sees clearly into that which is.)

### 40.

Everything deep loves masks; the deepest things have a veritable hatred of image and likeness. Might not *contrariety* be the only proper disguise to clothe the modesty of a god? A question worth asking. It would be surprising if some mystic hadn't at some time ventured upon it. There are events of such delicate nature that one would do well to bury them in gruffness and make them unrecognizable. There are deeds of love and extravagant magnanimity after which nothing is more advisable than to take a stick and beat up the eye-witness of them, to cloud his memory. There are people who know how to cloud and abuse their own memories in order to get revenge on their sole accomplice: modesty is inventive. The things of which one is most ashamed are by no means the worst things; not only cunning is found beneath a mask; there is much goodness in guile. I could imagine that a man who had something precious and vulnerable to hide might roll through life rough and round like an old green heavily hooped wine cask: the subtlety of his modesty would demand it. The destinies and delicate decisions of a man who is deeply ashamed happen to him on paths that few ever reach and of whose existence his nearest and dearest must know nothing. The danger to his life is hidden from their eyes, as is his life-security when he regains it. Such a concealed one, who instinctively uses speech for silence and withholding, and whose excuses for not communicating are inexhaustible, *wants* and encourages a mask of himself to wander about in the hearts and minds of his friends. And if he doesn't want it, one day his eyes will be opened to the fact that the mask is there anyway, and that it is good so. Every deep thinker needs a mask; even more, around every deep thinker a mask constantly grows, thanks to the continually wrong, i. e. superficial, interpretations of his every word, his every step, his every sign of life.—

### 41.

One must test oneself to see if one is meant for independence and for command. And one must do it at the right time. Never avoid your tests, though they may be the most dangerous game you can play, and in the end are merely tests at which you are the only witness and the sole judge. Never remain tied up with a person—not even the most beloved. Every person is a prison and a tight corner. Never remain tied up with a fatherland—not even when it most suffers and needs help (it is somewhat less difficult to untie one's heart for a victorious fatherland). Never remain tied up with compassion—not even compassion for a superior human being into whose rare torture and helplessness chance has given us an insight. Nor with a science, not even if it lures us with the most precious findings that seem to have been stored up for us alone. Never remain tied up with our own emancipation, that delicious bird-like distance and strangeness which soars ever higher and sees more and more spread out below; the danger of things that fly. Nor with our own virtues which would sacrifice the whole of us to some one thing, to our hospitality, for example. This is the danger of dangers to superior and lavish souls who spend themselves extravagantly and almost indifferently, turning the virtue of liberality into a vice. One must know how to *conserve* oneself. That is the most rigorous test of independence.

### 42.

A new species of philosopher is coming up over the horizon. I risk baptizing them with a name that is not devoid of peril. As I read them (as they allow themselves to be read—for it is characteristic of their type that they wish to remain riddles in some sense), these philosophers of the future have a right (perhaps also a wrong!) to be called: *Experimenters.*[2] This name itself is only an experiment, and, if you will, a temptation.

### 43.

Will they be new friends of "truth," these coming philosophers? Most probably, for all philosophers thus far have loved their truths. But surely they will not be dogmatists. It must run counter to their pride and their taste that their truth should be a truth for everyman, this having been the secret wish and ultimate motive of all dogmatic striving. "My judgment is *my* judgment, to which hardly anyone else has a right," is what the philosopher of the future will say. One must get rid of the bad taste of wishing to agree with many others. "Good" is no longer good in the mouth of my neighbor. And how could there be a "common good"! The expression contradicts itself: what can be common cannot have much value. In the end it must be as it

[2] The German word for attempt, tempt, and experiment is *versuchen.* Nietzsche here explicitly and elsewhere implicitly puns on it. *Translator.*

always was: great things remain for the great; abysses for the deep; delicacies and tremors for the subtle; and, all in all, all things rare for the rare!—

## 44.

After all this need I say especially that they shall be free, *very* free thinkers, these philosophers of the future? It is certain, however, that they will not be merely free thinkers but something more, something superior, greater, and thoroughly different, something that does not want to be misjudged or mistaken for something else. But, as I am saying this, I feel the *obligation* (almost as much toward them as toward ourselves, who are their heralds and fore-runners, we free thinkers) to blow away from all of us an old stupid prejudice and misunderstanding which for too long a time has made the concept "free thinker" opaque, like a fog. In all the countries of Europe and in America there is something nowadays which abuses this concept. There is a very narrow, im-prisoned, enchained sort of thinker who wants ap-proximately the opposite of our intentions and in-stincts, not to mention that in reference to the *new* philosophers coming up this sort would have to be a closed window and a bolted door. They belong, to make it short and sad, among the *levellers,* these falsely named "free thinkers." They are glib-tongued and scribble-mad slaves of democratic taste and its "modern ideas"; all of them are men without solitude, without solitude of their own; rough and ready boys to whom we cannot deny courage or respectable conduct but of whom we must say that they are unfree and ab-surdly superficial, especially in their basic inclination to see the cause for *all* human misery and failure in the structure of society as it has been up to now. This about turns the truth upside down. What they would like to strive for with all their power is the universal green pasture-happiness of the herd: security, lack of danger, comfort and alleviation of life for everyone. Their most frequently repeated songs and doctrines are "equal rights" and "compassion for all that suffers." Suffering is taken by them to be something that must be *abolished*. We opposed thinkers, who have opened our eyes and our consciences to the question, "How and where has the plant 'man' flourished most strongly so far?", we imagine that it has happened every time under the opposite conditions: that the peril of man's position had to grow to enormity; that his power of invention and dissembling (his "mind") had to develop subtlety and boldness under long pressure and compulsion; that his life-will had to be stepped up to an unconditional power-will. We imagine that hardness, violence, slavery, peril in the street and in the heart, concealment, Stoicism, temptation, and deviltry of every sort, everything evil, frightful, tyrannical, brutal, and snake-like in man, serves as well for the advancement of the species "man" as their opposite. In fact we are not even saying enough when we say this much. At any rate, with our speech and our silence, we have arrived at the *other* end of all modern ideologies and herd-desires. Perhaps we are their antipodes. No wonder that we "free thinkers" are not exactly the most communicative of thinkers. No wonder that we do not want to reveal in every particular what a mind can be made free *from,* and *to* what it might feel driven. As for the dangerous formula "beyond good and evil" which at least keeps us from being mistaken for someone else, we *are* something different from *"libres-penseurs," "liberi pensatori,"* "free-

thinkers," and whatever else these good proponents
of "modern ideas" like to be called. At home, or at
least a guest, in many lands of the spirit; escaped
many times from the stuffy pleasant corners into
which preference and prejudice, youth, origin, accidental meetings with men and books, or even the
weariness of our wanderings have seemed to pin us
down; full of malice against the bait of dependence
that lies hidden in honors or money or offices or
sensuous enthusiasms; grateful even for distress and
vicissitudinous disease because it always frees us from
some kind of a rule and its "prejudice"; grateful to
God, the devil, the sheep and the worm in us; curious
to a fault; investigative to the point of cruelty; with
impetuous fingers for the impalpable; with teeth and
stomachs for the indigestible; ready for any trade
demanding sharp-wittedness and sharp wits; ready
for any venture thanks to an excess of "free will";
with fore-souls and back-souls whose ultimate intentions are not easily fathomed; with foregrounds and
backgrounds that no foot can explore to the end;
concealed beneath cloaks of light; conquerors, though
we may look like inheritors and wastrels; arrangers
and collectors from early till late; misers of our
wealth and our full stuffed drawers; economical in
learning and forgetting; inventive of schemes; occasionally proud of tables of categories; occasionally
pedantic; occasionally night owls of work in the midst
of daylight; scarecrows, even, when necessary—and
today it is necessary insofar as we are the born,
sworn, jealous friends of *solitude,* our own deepest
midnight and mid-day solitude: this is the type of
man we are, we free thinkers! And perhaps *you* too,
you coming *new* philosophers, perhaps you too belong to this type.

# THIRD ARTICLE

## THE PECULIAR NATURE OF RELIGION

### 45.

The human psyche and its limits, the hitherto attained extent of human inner experience, the heights, depths, and distances of this experience, the entire history of the psyche up to now plus its still unexhausted possibilities: this is the hunting reservation for a born psychologist, for a passionate huntsman. But how often he must exclaim despairingly, "An individual—alas, only an individual—and faced with this huge primeval forest!" And so he desires several hundred assistants and subtle, educated hounds, whom he could drive into the history of the human psyche to drive *his* game together for him. In vain; it is proved on him again and again, thoroughly and bitterly, how impossible it is to find assistants and hounds for the very things which stimulate his curiosity. The difficulty with sending intellectuals into new and dangerous hunting domains is this: where courage, shrewdness and subtlety in every sense are most needed, just where the "big hunt," the big danger, begins—they cannot be used. At just that point they lose their trained eyes and noses. In order to read and determine, for example, the history of the problem of *consciousness* and *conscience* in the psyche of the *homines religiosi,* one would have to be as deep, as hurt, as monstrous, as the intellectual conscience of a Pascal. And besides, there would still be needed that vaulted heaven of bright malicious intelligence which is capable of viewing, ordering, and compelling into a formula this swarm of dangerous and painful experiences as one would see them from above. But who is there who could perform such a service for me? And who has time to wait for such a servant? They obviously grow too rarely; at all times they are so improbable! In the end one must do everything oneself in order to know a little bit oneself. That means, one has *much* to do. But a curiosity of my sort does remain one of the most pleasant vices. I beg your pardon, I meant to say, love for truth has its reward in heaven and even on earth.——

### 46.

Faith such as early Christianity demanded and not seldom attained, in the midst of a skeptical and southern-freethinking world which had behind it and within it centuries of struggle among the various philosophical schools, not counting the education for tolerance which the *imperium romanum* fostered— such faith was *not* the ingenuous and grumpy submission-faith with which a Luther or a Cromwell or some other Northern barbarian of the spirit cleaved to his God and his Christianity. It was more like that faith of Pascal's which looks in a horrible way like continuous suicide of the reason, a tough, long-lived, worm-like reason which cannot be killed at one time and with one blow. From the very beginning, the Christian faith is a sacrifice, sacrifice of all freedom, all pride, all self-assurance of the mind; at the same time it is servitude, self-mockery and self-mutilation. There is cruelty and religious Phoenician-ism in this faith which is expected of a worn-out many-faceted and much indulged conscience. Its presupposition is that the submission of the mind should *hurt* indescribably; that the entire past experience and habit of such a mind should defend itself against the *absurdissimum* which meets it in the guise of "the faith." Modern men, with their blunted sense for all Christian terminology, no longer feel the gruesome-superlative quality that lay for antique taste in the paradoxical formula "God on the cross." Nowhere and never hitherto has there been a similar boldness of reversal, anything similarly frightful, questioning and questionable, as this formula. It promised the re-valuation of all the values of antiquity. It is the Orient, the *deep* Orient, the Oriental slave, that took its revenge in this fashion against Rome and Rome's distinguished and frivolous tolerance, against Roman "catholicism" of unbelief. It was never faith but freedom from faith, a half-stoic and smiling care-lessness about the serious nature of faith in their master or masters that revolted the slaves. "Enlight-enment" is what revolts, for the slave wants an abso-lute; he understands only tyranny, even in morality; he loves, as he hates, without nuance, right to his depths, to the point of pain and disease. His great *concealed* suffering is revolted by the distinguished taste which seems to *deny* suffering. Skepticism as to suffering, basically merely an attitude of aristocratic morality, is not the least cause of the last great slave-revolt that began with the French Revolution.

### 47.

Wherever on earth the religious neurosis has ap-peared, it has been bound up with three dangerous dietary restrictions: solitude, fasting, and sexual ab-stinence. Still, it cannot be decided with certainty what is cause and what is effect and *whether* there is a cause-effect relationship at all. We are justified in this latter doubt because we know that one of the

most regular symptoms of savage as well as tame
peoples is an extremely sudden, extravagant sensuality which reverses itself, equally suddenly, into
paroxysms of penitence, utter negation of world and
will. Perhaps we might explain both phenomena as
a masked epilepsy. But we should disclaim explana-
tions nowhere more than here. There is not another
type whose interpretation has produced such an
abundance of nonsense and superstition; nothing else
seems to have interested people and even philosophers
more keenly. It is really time to grow a little cold, to
learn caution, or, even better, to look away and *step
aside*. In the background of even the most recent
philosophy, that of Schopenhauer, there still stands,
almost as *the* problem, this frightful question mark of
the religious crisis and awakening. How is negation
of the will *possible?* How is the saint possible? That
really seems to have been the question which made
Schopenhauer become a philosopher. And so it was
a truly Schopenhauerian consequence when his most
convinced disciple Richard Wagner (perhaps also the
last disciple, so far as Germany is concerned) con-
cluded his own life work at just this point. In the
end he presented on the stage that terrible everlasting
type, the *type vécu* as it lives and breathes, in the
form of Kundry. And at the same time the psychia-
trists of almost all the European countries were
having good cause to study the type close-up, everywhere that the religious neurosis (or "the peculiar
nature of religion," as I call it) was having its last
epidemic outbreak and parade in the form of the
"Salvation Army."—But if we ask ourselves just what
in the phenomenon of the saint has so irresistibly interested men of all types and all times, including the
philosophers, then we see that it is doubtless the

semblance of miraculousness that adheres to the
saint. By this I mean the immediate *succession of
antitheses,* of conditions of the psyche that are evaluated as morally antithetical. Out of a "bad man"
suddenly grows a "saint," a good man: this is what
seems suddenly palpable to us. Psychology heretofore
was shipwrecked at this point. Didn't this happen
mainly because psychology had placed itself beneath
the rule of morality, because itself *believed* in the
moral value-antitheses? And because it *read* these
antitheses into the text and the facts? Really? The
"miracle" might be only a fault of interpretation? A
lack of philological skill?—

## 48.

It seems that the Latin races are more inwardly
attached to their Catholicism than we Northerners
are to Christianity as a whole; that consequently unbelief in Catholic countries is something entirely different from unbelief in Protestant countries. With
them it is a sort of revolt against the spirit of the
race, with us more a return to the spirit (or ghost!)
of the race. We Northerners indubitably spring from
barbaric races, particularly in respect to our talent
for religion: we are poorly talented in this respect.
The Celts are an exception; they presented the best
soil for the growth of the Christian infection in the
North. In France the Christian ideal, insofar as the
pale Northern sun permitted it, reached its efflorescence. How foreignly pious for our taste are even
the last French skeptics when they have some Celtic
blood in their origins. How Catholic, how un-German
smells to our noses Auguste Comte's sociology with
its Roman logic of the instincts. How jesuitical that
charming and clever cicerone of Port Royal, Sainte-

Beuve, despite all his hostility to Jesuits. Not to speak of Ernest Renan—how inaccessible to us Northerners does the language of a Renan sound. At any given moment the merest bubble—a nothing, really—of religious tension throws his soul off balance, his voluptuous (in a refined sense) and comfortably stretched out soul! Just repeat some of these beautiful sentences after him and observe what malice and impertinence immediately stir in our probably less beautiful and much harder, that is to say, more German soul, in answer to him:

*Disons donc hardiment que la religion est un produit de l'homme normal, que l'homme est le plus dans le vrai quand il est le plus religieux et le plus assuré d'une destinée infinie. . . . C'est quand il est bon qu'il veut que la vertu corresponde à un ordre éternel, c'est quand il contemple les choses d'une manière désintéressée qu'il trouve la mort revoltante et absurde. Comment ne pas supposer que c'est dans ces moments-là, que l'homme voit le mieux?"* [1]

These sentences are so *antipodal* to my ears and my habits that when I first found them, my wrath wrote on the margin: *La niaserie religieuse par excellence!* [2] But my final, revised wrath grew to love them, these sentences with their truth upside down. It is so pleasant, so distinguished, to have one's own antipodes!

---

[1] Let us then say boldly that religion is a product of the normal man; that man is nearest to truth when he is most religious and most confident of a boundless destiny. . . . It is when he is good that he wishes virtue to correspond to an eternal order; it is when he looks disinterestedly at things that he finds death revolting and absurd. How then can we fail to assume that it is at such moments that he sees most clearly.

[2] Religious simple-minded nonsense of the highest order!

### 49.

What is astonishing about the religiosity of the ancient Greeks is the lavish abundance of gratitude that radiates from it. Only a very distinguished type of human being stands in *that* relation to nature and to life. Later, when the rabble came to rule in Greece, *fear* choked out religion and prepared the way for Christianity.

### 50.

The passion for God: it has its peasant-like, ingenuous, importunate types, like Luther. All of Protestantism lacks the Southern *delicatezza*. Then there is an Oriental self-alienation, as of a slave undeservedly granted mercy or exalted, like Augustine for example, who in a manner insulting to us lacks all distinction of gesture and desires. Then there is a womanly tenderness and ardor that modestly impelled toward an *unio mystica et physica* without knowing what it would mean, such as that of Madame de Guyon. In many cases it appears strangely enough in the guise of a maiden's or a youth's puberty; here and there even as the hysteria of an old maid; also as her ultimate ambition. Not infrequently the Church has canonized such a woman.

### 51.

Heretofore the mightiest of men have bowed in reverence before the saint, as the riddle of self-control and intentional ultimate abstinence. Why did they bow? They intuited in the saint (behind the question mark, as it were, of his fragile and miserable appearance) the superior power that was testing and proving itself with the self-control, the strength of will, in which they recognized and honored their own strength and pleasure in dominating. By honoring the saint they honored something in themselves. To this was added that the contemplation of the saint instilled in them a suspicion. Such an enormity of negation, of un-naturalness is surely not being desired for nothing, they asked and told themselves. Perhaps there is a reason, a very great danger, of which the ascetic has inside knowledge, thanks to his secret condolers and visitors. Enough, the mighty of the earth learned a new fear from the ascetic; they intuited a new power, a foreign, as yet unconquered enemy. It was their "will to power" that made them halt before the saint. They had something to ask him. . . .

### 52.

In the Jewish "Old Testament," the book of divine justice, there are men and things and speeches in such a grand style that Greek and Indic literature has nothing to equal them. One stands in awe and reverence before these enormous remains of what man once had been, and one has sad thoughts about ancient Asia and its tiny promontory Europe which insists on distinguishing itself by way of "human progress" from Asia. On the other hand: whoever is only a scrawny, tame, domestic animal with the needs of a domestic animal (like our "cultured" men of today, including the Christians of cultured Christendom), has nothing to surprise nor distress him when he views these ruins. One's taste for the Old Testament is a touchstone as to "great" and "small." Per-

haps the cultured man of today will find the New
Testament, the book of grace, much more in accordance with his heart. (It has much of the regular,
tender-hearted, stuffy odor of the devotee and the
small soul.) To have pasted this New Testament (a
rococo-taste in every sense) together into one book
with the Old Testament, and to call this the "Bible,"
"The Book," is possibly the greatest recklessness and
"sin against the Holy Ghost" that literary Europe
has on its conscience.

### 53.

Why atheism today? The "Father" in God is
thoroughly refuted, likewise the "judge" and the
"rewarder." Also his "free will"—he does not hear
us, and even if he heard us he could not help. The
worst of it is that he seems to be incapable of communicating clearly. Is he unclear?—This is what I
have found out from many questions and conversa-
tions as to the cause of the decline of European
theism. It seems to me that the religious instinct is
growing powerfully but is rejecting theistic gratification with deep distrust.

### 54.

What, basically, is all modern philosophy doing?
Since Descartes (and more in spite of him than proceeding from his premises), all philosophers are as-
saulting the old concept of soul, under the pretence
of criticizing our subject and predicate concept. This
means an assault on the basic premise of Christian
doctrine. Modern philosophy, being epistemological
skepticism, is secretly or openly anti-Christian,
though by no means anti-religious. (But that is said
for subtle ears only). We used to believe in the "soul"

as we believed in grammar and the grammatical
subject; we used to say that "I" was the condition,
"think" the predicate that conditioned, and thinking
an activity for which a subject *had to be* thought of
as its cause. But then we tried, with admirable per-
sistence and guile, to see whether the reverse might
not perhaps be true. "Think" was now the condition,
"I" the thing conditioned, hence "I" only a synthesis
which was *created* by thinking. Kant basically wanted
to prove that the subject could not be proved by the
subject—nor the object either. The possibility of an
*illusory existence* of the individual subject (the
"soul") may not have been a thought foreign to him.
It is the same thought which has already existed as
an immense power on earth, in the form of Vedanta-
philosophy.

## 55.

There is a great ladder of religious cruelty. It has
many rungs, but three of them are of the greatest
importance. The first is the sacrifice of men to one's
God, perhaps those men in particular whom one
most loved. Among these are the first-born offerings
of all primitive religions, and also Emperor Tiberius'
sacrifice in the Mithras grotto on the Isle of Capri—
that most gruesome of all Roman anachronisms. The
second rung, attained in the moral period of mankind, is the sacrifice to one's god of one's strongest
instincts, one's "natural man." *That* sort of festive
joy gleams in the cruel eyes of the ascetics, the enthusiastic "anti-naturalists." And finally—what remains that could be sacrificed? Don't we in the end
have to sacrifice everything consolatory, holy, and
healing; all hope, all belief in invisible harmony, in
future blessedness and justice? Don't we have to

sacrifice God himself and idolize a rock, the forces
of stupidity, of gravity, fate, nothingness—all in order
to be sufficiently cruel to ourselves? To sacrifice God
for nothingness—this is the paradoxical mystery of
ultimate cruelty that remained in store for the generation now growing up. All of us know something
about it already.

### 56.

Whoever, like myself, has because of some unknown desire long struggled to think Pessimism to
a greater depth and to release it from the half-
Christian, half-German narrowness and simple-
mindedness with which it was exhibited during this
past century in the form of Schopenhauerian philosophy—whoever has really looked at the most world-
negating of all possible ways of thinking with Asiatic
and ultra-Asiatic eyes—truly beyond good and evil
and no longer, like Buddha and Schopenhauer, under
the spell and illusion of morality—such a man has
perhaps had his eyes opened, even without having
wanted it, to the opposite ideal, the ideal of the truly
exuberant, alive, and world-affirming man who does
not merely resign himself to and learn to get along
with all that was and is, but who wants everything
*as it was and is* back again, back forever and ever,
insatiably calling *da capo,* not only to himself but to
the whole spectacle and performance, and not only
to the performance but basically to that which necessitates and needs the performance because it forever
and ever necessitates and needs itself! What did we
say? Is this not the *circulus vitiosus deus?*

### 57.

With man's power of spiritual sight and insight,

the distance—the space as it were—that surrounds him, grows. His world grows deeper; ever new stars, ever new riddles and constellations swim into his ken. Perhaps everything that trained the eyes of his mind to sharp-sightedness and insight was merely an excuse for the training itself, a learning game, a something for children and for childish minds. Perhaps some day the solemn concepts about which we struggled and suffered most, the concepts "God" and "sin," will appear no more important to us than a child's toy or a child's grief appears to an old man. And then perhaps the "old man," mankind, will need another toy and another grief—still enough of a child himself, forever and ever a child!

## 58.

Has it been properly noted to what extent external idleness or semi-idleness is necessary for a truly religious life (not only for its favorite microscopic work of self-examination but also for that delicate relaxation that calls itself "prayer" and is the constant readiness for the "coming of God")? And I mean idleness with a good conscience from time immemorial, a hereditary idleness, one related to the aristocratic feeling that work is *disgraceful* because it vulgarizes mind and body. And has it been noted that the modern, hustling, time-consuming, proud (stupidly proud) "hard work" ideal does more than anything else to educate and prepare man for unbelief? Among those, for example, who nowadays in Germany live remote from religion, I find men of all sorts and origins of "freethinking," but mostly a majority of those in whom generations of hard work have dissolved the religious instincts. They do not even know any longer what religions are good for;

they merely register their existence in the world with
a sort of dull astonishment. These good people feel
that their time is already sufficiently taken up by their
business and recreation—not to mention their "fatherland," their newspapers, and their "family duties." It
seems that they have no time left over for religion,
especially since it isn't clear to them whether religion
comes under the head of business or of pleasure. For
surely, they tell themselves, one does not attend
Church merely to spoil one's good humor! They are
not hostile to religious customs. If there are certain
demands (by the government, for example) for their
participation in such customs, they comply, as they
do with so much else, in patient, unassuming earnestness, without much curiosity or discomfort. They
simply live too much apart from and outside of religion to need so much as a "pro" or a "con" within
themselves. The majority of German middle-class
Protestants today belong to this indifferent group,
particularly in the great hard-working centers of trade
and commerce; likewise the majority of hard-working
intellectuals and the whole rest of the population of a
university-community (with the exception of the
theologians whose existence and possible existence
presents an ever more subtle riddle to the psychologists). Pious or even church-going people today
seldom have a conception of *how* much good will
(one could say voluntary will) it takes for a German
intellectual to treat the problem of religion as a
serious one. His whole trade (his whole hard-working
workman-like nature, as I have said, to which his
modern conscience obligates him) inclines him to a
superior, almost kind-hearted, amiability toward religion. This is occasionally mixed with a faint disdain
for the "uncleanness" of spirit which he supposes

wherever the church is still acknowledged. Only with the help of history (hence *not* through personal experience) does the intellectual succeed in confronting the religions with a respectful seriousness and a certain shame-faced consideration. But even where his feeling has been elevated to the point of gratitude toward religion, his person has not advanced a single step toward whatever still exists of church and piousness—perhaps the contrary. The practice of indifference to things religious into which he is born and educated is usually sublimated into a circumspection and cleanliness that disinclines him to any contact with religious men and things. It can be precisely the depth of his tolerance and humanity that bids him avoid the delicate necessities brought on by toleration. Each period has its own divine methods of naïveté whose invention might well be the envy of other periods. And how much naive, respect-worthy, child-like, and boundlessly asinine naïveté, lies in the intellectual's belief in his own superiority, in the good conscience of his tolerance, in the unsuspecting, homely self-confidence with which his instinct looks down on the religious man as an inferior and lower type. He imagines that he himself has surpassed it, risen beyond and *above* it—he, the puny, pretentious dwarf and "common man," the assiduously astute brain-worker, the handy-man of ideas—of modern ideas!

### 59.

Who has looked deep into the world can well understand the wisdom that lies in the fact that men are superficial. It is their instinct for self-preservation that teaches them to take things lightly, to skim over the surface, to be false. Here and there one can find a passionate and exaggerated adoration of "pure form," in philosophers and in artists. Let no one doubt that anyone who *needs* that kind of cult of surface-things has at some time or other unhappily reached *beneath* the surface. Perhaps there is an order or rank, even, in these burnt children, these born artists who can find pleasure in life only in their intention to *counterfeit* its image (to take slow revenge on life, as it were). One might deduce the degree to which they are sick of life from the degree to which they desire to see its image counterfeited, attenuated, transcendentalized, and deified. One might count the *homines religiosi* among these artists, assigning them the highest rank. It is deep, suspicious fear of incurable pessimism that forces whole millenniums to sink their teeth into a religious interpretation of life. It is that fearful instinct which intuits that man might come into possession of the truth *too soon,* before he has grown strong enough, hard enough, artist enough. Looked at in this light, piety, "living in God," would appear to be the subtlest and ultimate product of the *fear* of truth. It would appear to be the artist's adoration of and intoxication with the most consistent of all counterfeitings, the will to the reversal of truth, to untruth at any cost. Perhaps there has heretofore been no stronger medicine for beautifying man than piety. Through piety, man can become so much of a work of art, of surface, of color-play, and goodness, that one no longer suffers whenever one looks at him.

### 60.

To love mankind *for God's sake* has up to now been the most distinguished and far-fetched feeling that mankind has reached. That love for mankind, without some sanctifying reservation, is only *one more* stupidity and brutishness, that the impulse to such love must first get its proportion, its delicacy, its grain of salt and dash of ambergris from a higher impulse—whatever man first felt and underwent ("experienced") this, however his tongue may have stammered as it attempted to express such a fragile matter, let him for all time be held holy and worthy of respect. For he was the man who has flown higher, and lost his way more beautifully, than anyone else. . . .

### 61.

The philosopher, as we free thinkers understand him, the man with the most extensive responsibility, whose conscience must do for the total development of mankind, this philosopher will use religions for his educational and training purposes, just as he uses the political and economic institutions of his time. The selective, cultivating influence (which always implies destruction as well as creation and form-giving) that can be exerted with the help of the religions varies considerably with the type of men who are placed beneath its spell and protection. For strong, independent men, prepared and predestined for command, in whom is incarnated the reason and the art of a ruling race, religion is one more instrument for overcoming obstacles, for being able to rule. It is a bond which binds rulers and ruled alike and reveals to the rulers the conscience of the ruled, their hidden and innermost parts which would like to escape obedience, and delivers itself up to them. And in case individual personalities of distinguished origin incline because of a high degree of spirituality toward a more contemplative life apart, reserving for themselves only the subtlest type of ruling (over select disciples or monastic brothers), religion can even be used as an instrument for creating some peace for oneself from the noise and trouble of coarser rule, and cleanliness to guard against the *inevitable* dirt of all politicking. This is what the Brahmins did with religion; with the aid of a religious organization they gave themselves the power to nominate the kings of their people, but they held and felt themselves to be apart from and outside of the government, as men of higher and supra-regal tasks. Meanwhile religion also provides guidance to a section of the ruled, giving them an opportunity to prepare themselves for later rule and command. These are the slowly ascending strong classes and castes in whom, through fortunate marriage customs, will power and pleasure in will power, that is, the will to self-control, is ever rising. To these, religion offers enough opportunities and temptations to walk the paths of superior spirituality, to try out their feeling for self-control in the widest sense, for silence, and for solitude. Asceticism and Puritanism are almost indispensable means for the education and ennoblement of a race that seeks to rise above its origin in the masses and is working toward eventual leadership. To ordinary people, finally, to the great majority who exist to serve the general welfare (and who *should* exist only for this), religion gives an invaluable contentedness with their situation and their type, manifold peace of heart, an ennobling of their obedience, one more joy and grief to share with their peers, and something that transfigures and beautifies them, something that justifies the every-day quality of their life, their inferiority, and the whole half-animal poverty of their soul. Reli-

gion and the religious significance of life lay an aura
of sunshine on such forever plagued people; it makes
their own sight endurable for them; it has the effect
on them that Epicureanism usually has on sufferers
of a higher order—it refreshes, refines, it *utilizes,* as
it were, their suffering; in the end it sanctifies and
justifies them. Perhaps nothing in Christianity and
Buddhism is so worthy of respect as their skill in
teaching even the lowest that they can be included
in a higher illusionary order of things through piety.
This enables the religion to keep them satisfied to
remain in the real order in which they find it difficult
enough to live—but precisely this difficulty is
necessary!

## 62.

Finally, to be sure, we must draw up the wicked
counter-evidence that these religions present and so
bring to light their uncanny dangerousness. One
must always pay dearly and frightfully when religions
do *not* operate as a cultivating and educating force
in the hands of philosophers, but rule sovereign and
cut-off; when they want to be ultimate ends in themselves instead of means among other means. Mankind, like any other animal species, produces an
excess of abortive, diseased, degenerate, defective,
and necessarily suffering specimens; the successful
specimens, in men as well, are always the exception.
And considering that man is *the not yet stabilized*
animal, they are the rare exception. Even worse, the
higher the type of which an individual is a specimen,
the greater the improbability of his *turning out well.*
The forces of chance, the law of nonsense in the total
economy of mankind, shows up most horrifyingly in
its destructive effect on the superior individuals whose

proper life conditions are subtle, manifold, and difficult to calculate. Now what is the conduct of the two above mentioned great religions toward the *excess* of defective specimens? They seek to maintain, to retain for life, what can possibly be retained; they principally side with the defectives, being religions *for sufferers;* they confirm the rights of all those who suffer from life as though it were a disease; they would like to render invalid and impossible any other sentiment besides theirs. No matter how justly and carefully we evaluate this protective and preservative care (which in addition to all the others applies to the highest type of man who also belongs to the greatest sufferers), it nonetheless remains that in the total reckoning the present, *sovereign* religions are among the main causes that have held mankind as a type down to a lower level. They preserved too much of what *should have perished.* We have an *inestimable* debt of gratitude to them; who is there so rich in gratitude that he would not grow poor when he thinks of all that the "spiritual men" of Christendom, for example, have done for Europe! And yet— if they gave consolation to the suffering, courage to the oppressed and despairing, a staff and a support to the dependent; if they lured the inwardly ravaged and savage away from society and into monasteries and psychic reformatories—what else must they not have done to work thus, principally, with a clear conscience, on the preservation of the diseased and the suffering, indeed and in truth, on the *deterioration of the European race!* To turn upside down all valuations—*that* is what they had to do! To shatter the strong, to infect great hopes, to cast suspicion on the enjoyment of beauty, to break down everything autonomous, manly, victorious, dominating, all the instincts natural to the highest and best turned-out type of mankind, and bend it over into uncertainty, distress of conscience, and self-destruction—to reverse every bit of love for the earth and things earthly and control of the earth into hatred of things earthly and of the earth: *this* was the self-assumed task of the church. And it considered this task necessary until, by its own standards, "unworldliness" and "de-sensualization" and "superior man" finally melted together into a single feeling. If one could have an over-all view of the strangely painful comedy of European Christendom, as coarse as it is subtle, and view it with the mocking and non-participant eye of an Epicurean god, one would, I think, forever remain astonished and unable to stop laughing. For doesn't it seem as though one single will had controlled Europe for eighteen centuries—the will to create a *sublime abortion* out of mankind? But if one's need were reversed, if one were not an Epicurean, but stepped up to this almost voluntary degeneration and stunting of man that the European Christian (Pascal, for example) presents, if one confronted it with some kind of divine hammer in one's hand, wouldn't one have to shout in anger and compassion and horror: Oh, you bungling fools, you presumptuous compassionate fools—what have you done? Was this a work for *your* hands? How have you hacked up and botched my beautiful stone! How dare *you* mess!— What I meant to say was that Christianity has heretofore been the most fateful example of presumptuous self-estimation. Men who were not superior and rigorous enough to work *on mankind* in the way artists must work, men who were not strong and far-sighted enough, who did not have enough sublime self-control to *allow* the preliminary law of thousandfold failures and mortalities to operate, men who were not distinguished enough to see the abysmally different orders of rank and the distances between ranks in man—*such* men have heretofore administered the fate of Europe with their "equality before God," until they have managed to cultivate a wizened, almost ludicrous type, a herd-animal, a creature compounded of good will, sickliness, and mediocrity: the European of today. . . .

# FOURTH ARTICLE

## APHORISMS AND ENTR'ACTES

### 63.

Whoever is fundamentally a teacher takes things —including himself—seriously only as they affect his students.

### 64.

"Insight for its own sake" is the ultimate snare that morality sets for us. We shall be completely entangled in it one day.

### 65.

The charm of insight would be small if there were not so much modesty to overcome on the way.

### 65a.

One is most dishonest toward one's God: he is not *permitted* to sin!

### 66.

The inclination to lower himself, to let himself be stolen from, lied to, and exploited, could be the modesty of a god who walks among men.

### 67.

Love for any one thing is barbaric, for it is exercised at the expense of everything else. This includes the love for God.

### 68.

"I did this," says my memory. "I cannot have done

this," says my pride, remaining inexorable. Eventually, my memory yields.

### 69.

One has not watched life very observantly if one has never seen the hand that—kills tenderly.

### 70.

If one has character, one has also one's typical experience that recurs again and again.

### 71.

*The wise man as astronomer:* As long as you feel the stars to be "above" you, you do not gaze as one who has insight.

### 72.

Not the strength but the permanence of superior sensibilities is the mark of the superior man.

### 73.

Who reaches his ideal thereby surpasses it.

### 73a.

There is many a peacock who hides his tail from all eyes—and calls it his pride.

### 74.

A man of genius is unbearable if he does not have at least two other things: gratitude and cleanliness.

### 75.

The degree and the type of a man's sexuality reaches to the highest peaks of his spirit.

### 76.

When there is peace, the warlike man attacks himself.

### 77.

One uses one's principles to tyrannize or justify or honor or affront or conceal one's habits. Two men with similar principles may easily want totally different things with them.

### 78.

Whoever despises himself still esteems the despiser within himself.

### 79.

A soul who knows it is loved but does not love back reveals its sediment: it is turned completely bottom side up.

### 80.

A matter which has come to light ceases to matter to us. What did that god mean who advised man to "know thyself"? Did he mean "Cease to matter to yourself! Become objective!"? And what about Socrates? And the "scientist"?

### 81.

It is terrible to die of thirst at sea. Must you salt your truth so heavily that it cannot even any longer —quench thirst?

### 82.

"Compassion for all" would amount to rigor and tyranny for *you*, my dear neighbor!

### 83.

*Instinct:* When the house is on fire one forgets even the dinner.—Yes, but one goes to the ashes to eat it.

### 84.

A woman learns to hate in proportion as she unlearns how to enchant.

### 85.

The same passions in man and woman nonetheless differ in tempo; hence man and woman do not cease misunderstanding one another.

### 86.

Behind all their personal vanity, women still impersonally despise "woman."

### 87.

*Heart in bond, spirit free.* When one places one's heart in firm bonds and keeps it locked up, one can afford to give one's spirit many liberties. I already said this once. But people do not believe me—unless they know it already. . . .

### 88.

One begins to distrust very clever people when they become embarrassed. . . .

### 89.

Terrible experiences give one cause to speculate whether the one who experiences them may not be something terrible.

### 90.

Grave, melancholy men grow lighter and at times reach their surface through just those things which make others grave: through hatred and through love.

### 91.

So cold, so icy, that one burns one's fingers on him! Every hand that touches him receives a shock. This is why some think he is burning hot.

### 92.

Who has not at some time or other sacrificed himself, in order to save his reputation?

### 93.

There is no misanthropy in affability, but all the more contempt.

### 94.

Man's maturity: to have regained the seriousness that he had as a child at play.

### 95.

To be ashamed of one's un-morality is a rung of the ladder at whose end one is also ashamed of one's morality.

### 96.

One should part from life as Odysseus parted from Nausicaa: with a blessing rather than in love.

### 97.

A great man, did you say? All I ever see is the actor creating his own ideal image.

### 98.

When we coach our conscience, it kisses us as it bites.

### 99.

*The disappointed one says:* I hoped for a response and heard merely praise. . . .

### 100.

We all pretend to ourselves that we are more simple-minded than we are: that is how we get a rest from our fellowmen.

### 101.

A man of insight nowadays might easily feel that he was God incarnate in a beast.

### 102.

When love is returned, it should really disenchant the lover with the beloved creature. "What? She is so modest in her demands as to love even you? Or so dumb? Or, or. . . ."

### 103.

*The danger in happiness:* Now everything I touch turns out to be wonderful. Now I love any fate that comes along. Who feels like being my fate?

### 104.

Not their love, but the impotence of their love keeps today's Christians from—burning us at the stake.

### 105.

For the free thinker, for one who has "piety of insight," a pious fraud is even harder to swallow than an impious fraud. It runs counter to *his* piety. Hence his deep lack of understanding for the church. Insofar as he belongs to the type "free thinker," he takes the church to be *his* lack of freedom.

### 106.

The passions enjoy themselves in the form of music.

### 107.

When the mind is made up, the ear is deaf to even the best arguments. This is the sign of a strong character. In other words, an occasional will to stupidity.

### 108.

There are no moral phenomena, only a moral interpretation of phenomena. . . .

### 109.

Frequently the criminal is not the equal of his crime. He belittles it and slanders it.

### 110.

Criminal lawyers are rarely artists enough to turn the beautifully horrible aspect of a crime to the advantage of the criminal.

### 111.

Our vanity is most difficult to wound when our pride has just been wounded.

### 112.

Whoever feels predestined for contemplation instead of faith finds all the faithful too noisy and obtrusive. He defends himself against them.

### 113.

You want him to be prejudiced in your favor? Then pretend you are embarrassed before him. . . .

### 114.

The enormous expectation that women have of sex, and the modesty involved in the expectation, spoils their perspective from the very beginning.

### 115.

Where love or hate have no share in the game, a woman's playing is mediocre.

### 116.

The great epochs of our lives come when we gain the courage to rebaptize our evil as our best.

### 117.

The will to overcome a passion is in the end merely the will of another or several other passions.

### 118.

There is an innocence in admiration. It is possessed by someone to whom it has not yet occurred that he, too, might be admired some day.

### 119.

Disgust at dirt can be so great that it keeps us

from cleaning ourselves up—from "justifying" ourselves.

### 120.

Sensuality often grows too fast for love to keep up with. Then love's root remains weak and is easily torn up.

### 121.

There is a subtlety in the fact that God learned Greek when he wanted to become an author—and that he didn't learn it any better.

### 122.

The enjoyment of praise is in some people merely a courtesy of the heart—the very opposite of vanity of the intellect.

### 123.

Concubinage, too, has been corrupted—by marriage.

### 124.

Whoever is joyous when burning at the stake is not triumphant over pain, but over the fact that there is no pain where he expected it. A parable.

### 125.

When we must change our minds about someone, we charge the inconvenience he causes us heavily to his account.

### 126.

A people is nature's detour to six or seven great

men. Yes, and then the means to get around even them.

### 127.

Science runs counter to the modesty of all genuine women. They feel as though it were being used to peek under their skins—worse yet, under their dress and make-up.

### 128.

The more abstract the truth you want to teach, the more thoroughly you must seduce the senses to accept it.

### 129.

The devil has the farthest perspectives for God— that is why he stays so far away from him. The devil, in other words, is the oldest friend of insight.

### 130.

What someone *is,* begins to be revealed when his talent abates, when he stops showing what he can *do.* Talent, too, is a form of cosmetics; cosmetics, too, are a hiding device.

### 131.

The sexes deceive themselves about one another. For fundamentally they honor and love only themselves (or their own ideal, to say it more pleasingly). Man, for example, wants woman to be peaceable, but women are unpeaceable *by their very nature,* like cats, however well they have trained themselves to appear peaceable.

### 132.

One is best punished for one's virtues.

### 133.

Who cannot find the way to his *own* ideal, lives more recklessly and impudently than a man without an ideal.

### 134.

Only from the senses comes all credibility, all clear conscience, all self-evidence of truth.

### 135.

Pharisaism is not a degeneracy of a good man; on the contrary, a large part of it is the necessary condition for being good.

### 136.

One person seeks a midwife for his thoughts; the other, someone he can assist. Here is the origin of a good conversation.

### 137.

When dealing with intellectuals and artists, one readily makes the opposite mistakes: beneath a remarkable intellectual there is often a mediocre man, but beneath a mediocre artist there is quite often a very remarkable man.

### 138.

What we do in our dreams we also do in our waking hours; we first invent and create the man with whom we are dealing and then—we forget immediately that we have done it.

### 139.

In revenge and in love, women are more barbaric than men.

### 140.

*Advice in the form of a riddle:* If you want the bond to hold, bite on it—free and bold.

### 141.

Man's belly is the reason why man does not easily take himself for a god.

### 142.

The chastest utterance I have heard: *"Dans le véritable amour c'est l'âme, qui enveloppe le corps."* [1]

### 143.

Our vanity would like to have it understood that what we do best comes hardest to us. A contribution toward the origin of many a morality.

### 144.

When a woman is intellectually inclined there is usually something wrong with her sex. Even barrenness disposes her to a certain masculinity of taste; for man—if I may say so—is the "barren animal."

### 145.

Comparing men and women as a whole, one may say that women would not have their genius for adornment if they did not have the instinct for playing a *secondary role*.

[1] In true love it is the soul that envelopes the body.

### 146.

Whoever battles with monsters had better see that it does not turn him into a monster. And if you gaze long into an abyss, the abyss will gaze back into you.

### 147.

This out of old Florentine *novellas*, and, incidentally, out of life: *buona femmina e mala femmina vuol bastone.* Sacchetti, *Nov.* 86.[2]

### 148.

To seduce their neighbor into thinking well of them, and then to believe implicitly in this opinion of their neighbor: who has greater skill in this than a woman?

### 149.

What a given period feels to be evil is usually the unseasonable echo of something that used to be felt as good—the atavism of an older ideal.

### 150.

Around the hero, all things turn into tragedy; around the demigod, into a satyr-play; and around God all things turn into—did you say, "world"?

### 151.

To have a talent is not enough for you; one must also have your permission to have it, eh, my friends?

### 152.

"Wherever the tree of knowledge stands is Paradise" say the oldest and the youngest serpents.

[2] Good women and bad women alike want to be beaten.

### 153.

What is done out of love always happens beyond good and evil.

### 154.

Objections, non-sequiturs, cheerful distrust, joyous mockery—all are signs of health. Everything absolute belongs in the realm of pathology.

### 155.

The sense for tragedy increases and decreases with sensuality.

### 156.

Insanity is the exception in individuals. In groups, parties, peoples, and times, it is the rule.

### 157.

The thought of suicide is a strong consolation; one can get through many a bad night with it.

### 158.

Not only our reason but our conscience succumbs to our strongest drive, to the tyrant within us.

### 159.

We *must* repay both good and ill—but not necessarily to the person who did us the good or ill.

### 160.

One no longer loves one's insight enough when one communicates it.

### 161.

Poets behave shamelessly toward their experiences: they exploit them.

### 162.

The fellow next to us is not our neighbor; the one next to *him* is. So thinks every nation.

### 163.

Love brings out the high and hidden qualities of the lover—his rare, exceptional states. Hence it easily deceives us about his ordinary ways, his "rule."

### 164.

Jesus said to his Jews, "The Law was made for servants. Love God, as I do, love him as a son does. What do we sons of God care about morality!"

### 165.

*Looking at any political party:* Every shepherd needs a bell-wether to lead his flock—or else he must be one.

### 166.

We may lie with our lips, but we tell the truth with the face we make when we lie.

### 167.

In rigorous men, tenderness is a matter for modesty —and something precious.

### 168.

Christianity gave Eros poison to drink; he did not die of it but he degenerated into vice.

### 169.

Talking much about oneself may be a way of hiding oneself.

### 170.

There is more obtrusiveness in praise than in blame.

### 171.

Compassion works on a man of insight almost to make him laugh—like tender hands laid on a Cyclops.

### 172.

For sheer love of humanity one occasionally embraces some random person (because one cannot embrace everyone). But this is the one thing one must not let the random person know. . . .

### 173.

One does not hate as long as one has a low esteem of someone, but only when one esteems him as an equal or a superior.

### 174.

You Utilitarians! You too love utility only as a wagon-cart to transport your inclinations. You too really find the creaking of its wheels unbearable—do you?

### 175.

Ultimately one loves one's desire, not the desired object.

## 176.

The vanity of others runs counter to our taste only when it runs counter to our vanity.

## 177.

Perhaps no one yet has been sufficiently truthful about the nature of "truthfulness."

## 178.

One does not believe in the follies of clever men— this is unfair to human rights!

## 179.

The consequences of our actions grab us by the back of the neck, blithely disregarding the fact that we have meanwhile "reformed."

## 180.

There is a kind of innocence in a lie which is the sign of good faith in a cause.

## 181.

It is inhuman to bless where one is being cursed.

## 182.

The familiarity of one's superior makes one bitter because it cannot be reciprocated.

## 183.

"What has shaken me is not that you lied to me but that I no longer believe you now. . . ."

### 184.

There is an impetuosity of goodness that looks like malice.

### 185.

"I don't like it." "Why not?" "Because I am not up to handling it." Did ever a man answer thus?

# FIFTH ARTICLE

## CONTRIBUTIONS TO THE NATURAL HISTORY OF MORALITY

### 186.

Moral sensibility in Europe today is just as subtle, ancient, manifold, sensitive, and refined as the "science of morality" that goes with it is young, raw, clumsy, and inept. This is a fascinating opposition which occasionally takes on color and flesh in the person of some moralist. The very expression, "science of morality," is much too arrogant and in bad taste for that which is designated by it. (Good taste being usually a pre-taste for more modest words.) One ought rigorously to admit *what* it is that will be necessary for a long time to come, *what* alone is justified now—namely the collection of the material, the conceptual formalization and arrangement of an enormous field of delicate value-feelings and value-differences which are living, growing, generating others, and perishing, and—possibly—some experiments to illustrate the more recurrent and frequent forms of this living crystallization. All this to prepare a *typology* of morality. Hitherto, to be sure, we have not been so modest. All the philosophers, with a stiff, ludicrous earnestness, demanded something much higher, more pretentious, more solemn of themselves, as soon as they dealt with morality as a science. What they wanted was to *establish the derivation* of morality, and each philosopher thought he had done so; morality itself he took to be "given."

How far from their brash pride lay the apparently insignificant task of description. It was left to collect dust and mold, when the subtlest hands and senses would hardly be subtle enough for it. Precisely because the moral philosophers knew the facts of morality only roughly, arbitrarily abstracted or randomly abbreviated (as the morality of their environment, for example, or their profession, or their church, or the spirit of their time, or their climate and continent), precisely because they were poorly informed and not very inquisitive about other peoples, epochs, and times—for these reasons they never even saw the real problems of morality. For the real problems only appear when one compares *many* moralities. All "science of morality" thus far lacked (peculiar as it may sound) the problem of morality itself; it lacked the suspicion that there was something problematical in morality. What the philosophers claimed for themselves and called "derivation of morality" was, seen in the proper light, only a learned form of good *faith* in the prevailing morality, only another means for expressing it—in other words only another piece of evidence of a given morality. Ultimately it was a sort of denial that this given morality *could* be looked upon as problematical. In any event, it was the converse of a testing, an analysis, a doubt, a vivisection of just this faith of theirs. Let us listen, for example, to the really remarkable innocence with which Schopenhauer assigns himself his task; let us draw our own conclusions about the scientific method of a "science" whose past masters talk like children or old biddies. "The principle," says Schopenhauer (on p. 137 of *Grundprobleme der Ethik*), "the axiom on which all ethical philosophers are *essentially* agreed, namely

*neminem laede, immo omnes, quantum potes, juva*[1]
—this is *essentially* the proposition which all teachers
of ethics strive to establish . . . the *essential* foundation of ethics which is being sought for millenniums
like the philosopher's stone." It may be indeed difficult to establish such a proposition as fundamental
—not even Schopenhauer succeeded in doing so, as
is well known. And if there is someone who has
fundamentally felt and agreed just how insipidly
false and sentimental this proposition is in a world
whose essence is will to power—let him remember
that Schopenhauer, though a pessimist, was "essentially" a flautist. . . . Daily, after dinner, his biog-
rapher tells us. Which raises the incidental question:
a pessimist, a negator of God and world, who *stops*
when confronted with morality, who says "yes" to
morality and tootles his flute to the tune of this
"injure-no-man-morality"—is such a man essentially
a pessimist?

## 187.

Aside from asking the value of certain assertions
such as "There is a categorical imperative in us,"
one may also ask what such an assertion tells of the
asserter. There are moralities which are supposed to
justify their originator in the eyes of other men; those
which are supposed to quiet him and resign him to
himself; those with which the originator wants to
crucify and humiliate himself; those with the help of
which he wants revenge; those with which to hide
himself or transfigure himself or put altitude and distance between himself and other men. One morality
helps its originator forget something; another mo-

[1] Injure no man, rather help all men so far as you are
able.

rality helps him or something about him to be forgotten. Some moralists want to exercise their power and creative caprice on mankind; others, Kant perhaps among them, want us to understand something like "What must be respected in me is my capacity for obedience and—*you shall not* be any better off than I am!" In short, moralities too are but a *symbolic language of the passions.*

## 188.

Every morality, in contrast to *laisser aller,* is a work of tyranny against "nature" and also against "reason." But this is not an objection to it—not unless one wished to decree (proceeding from some sort of morality) that all types of tyranny and irrationality are to be forbidden. What is essential and of inestimable value in each morality is that it is a long-lasting restraint. To understand Stoicism or Port-Royal or Puritanism, it is well to remember the restraints under which any language hitherto has reached its peak of power and subtlety—the restraint of metrics, the tyranny of rhyme and rhythm. How much trouble have the poets and orators of each nation always taken (not excepting several of today's prose writers) with an inexorable conscience in their ear, "for the sake of a folly" say the Utilitarian fools who think they are clever, "in deference to arbitrary laws" say the anarchists who imagine they are "free," in fact freethinkers. The strange fact, however, is that everything of freedom, subtlety, boldness, dance, and craftsmanlike certainty that one can find on earth, whether it applies to thinking, or ruling, or speaking, or persuading—in the arts as well as in codes of conduct—would never have developed save through the "tyranny of such arbitrary laws." Indeed, the probability is strong that *this* is "nature" and "natural"—and *not—laisser aller!* Every artist knows how far his most "natural" condition is from the feeling of letting oneself go, how rigorously and subtly he obeys a thousandfold law in the moments of "inspiration," in his free ordering, locating, disposing, and formgiving, how his laws mock at all formulation into concepts, precisely because they are so rigorous and well-defined (even the firmest concept, compared to them, has something teeming, manifold, and ambiguous about it). The essential thing "in heaven and on earth," it seems, is —to say it once more—that there be obedience, long continued obedience in some one direction. When this happens, something worthwhile always comes of it in the end, something which makes living worthwhile; virtue, for example, or art or music or dance or reason or spirituality—something that transfigures us, something subtly refined, or mad, or divine. The long bondage of the spirit, the long repression in the communicability of thoughts, the discipline assumed by the thinker to think within an ecclesiastical or court-imposed system or within the framework of Aristotelian assumptions, the enduring, intellectual will to interpret all that happens according to the Christian scheme, to discover and justify the Christian God in every accident—all this violence, arbitrariness, rigor, gruesomeness and anti-rationality turned out to be the means for disciplining the European spirit into strength, ruthless inquisitiveness, and subtle flexibility. We must admit, of course, that much which is irreplaceable in energy and spirit was suppressed, choked out, and ruined in this same process (for here, as everywhere, "nature" shows up as that which it is, in all its wasteful and *indifferent* magnificence which outrages us but which is a mark of its distinction). That European thinkers for millenniums thought only in order to prove something (today the case is reversed and we distrust any thinker who is out to prove something), that they always knew very definitely what was *supposed* to be the result of their most rigorous thinking (think of the example of Asiatic astrology or today's harmless Christian-moral interpretation of personal events as happening "to the greater glory of God" or "for the good of the soul"!)—all this tyranny, this arbitrariness, this rigorous and grandiose stupidity has *disciplined* and *educated* the spirit. It seems that slavery, in both its coarser and its finer application, is the indispensable means for even spiritual discipline and cultivation. Look at any morality—you will see that it is its "nature" to teach hatred of *laisser aller,* of too much freedom, and to implant the need for limited horizons, for the nearest task. It teaches the *narrowing of perspectives,* in other words stupidity in a certain sense, as a necessary condition for life and growth. "Thou shalt obey, someone or other, and for a long time; *if not,* you perish and lose your last self-respect"—this seems to me to be the moral imperative of nature. It is neither categorical, to be sure, as old Kant demanded (observe the "if not"!), nor is it directed to any individual. What does nature care about an individual! But it is directed to peoples, races, times, classes, and—above all—to the whole animal known as "man," to *mankind.*

### 189.

The hard-working races endure leisure only with great difficulty. It was a masterpiece of *British* in-

stinct to sanctify and dullify the Sunday to such a
degree that the Briton quite unnoticeably begins to
yearn for his workaday week. It is a type of cleverly
invented, cleverly interpolated *fasting,* the likes of
which are frequently found in the ancient world
(though, as is proper for Southern peoples, not in
reference to work—of all things). There must be
many kinds of fasting. Wherever powerful drives
and habits rule people, the law-givers have to see to
it that days are intercalated on which such a drive is
temporarily chained and thus learns to go hungry
again. From a higher point of view, whole generations and times that show up with some sort of
moral fanaticism seem to be such intercalated restraint and fasting periods during which a drive
learns to duck and submit, but also to *clean* and
*sharpen* itself. Certain philosophical sects as well
(the Stoa, for example, in the midst of Hellenic
culture and its over-ripe aphrodisiac air), permit of
such an interpretation. With this, an explanation is
hinted at of the paradox that it was only during the
Christian period of Europe, and under the pressure
of Christian value judgments, that sex sublimated
itself into love *(amour-passion)!*

### 190.

There is something in Plato's morality that does
not essentially belong to Plato but is merely found
in his philosophy—in spite of Plato, one might say.
This is Socratism, for which he was essentially too
distinguished. "No one wishes to do harm to himself;
hence everything bad happens involuntarily. For the
bad man harms himself; if he knew that the bad
was bad, he would not do it. Consequently the bad
man is bad only through error; if we deprive him of

his error, we necessarily make him—good." This
sort of logic smells of rabble, who see only the
miserable consequences of a bad act and who essentially judge that "it is *dumb* to do the bad,"
taking "good" without further ado to be synonymous
with "useful and pleasurable." One may, following
one's nose, guess at such an origin when one sees
any kind of moral utilitarianism. One will seldom
go wrong. Plato did everything he could to interpret
something subtle and distinguished into the proposition of his teacher; above all, he tried to interpret
himself into it—he, the most reckless of all interpre-
ters who took over the whole of Socrates as though
he were taking a popular theme or folksong from
the alley, in order to play his own variations on it,
past the limits of the finite and the possible, the variations of all his own masks and multiplicities. In jest,
and in Homeric language besides, what after all is
the Platonic Socrates if not

Ποόσδε Πλάτων ὄπιδέν τε Πλάτων μεσση τε Χίμαιοα.[2]

## 191.

The old theological problem of "faith" vs. "knowledge," or, more plainly, of instinct vs. reason—the
question, in other words, whether, in respect to valuation, instinct deserves a greater authority than
rationality which inquires for reasons, for a "why,"
hence demands valuations and acts in conformity
with purpose and utility—this problem is still the
old problem of morality that first arose in the person of Socrates and divided thinker from thinker

[2] Plato in front, Plato behind, a Chimaera in the
middle.

long before Christianity. Socrates himself had at first sided with reason, as befitted the taste of his talent (that of a superior dialectician); what, in fact, did he do all his life but laugh at the inept inabilities of his distinguished Athenians who were men of instinct like all distinguished human beings and could never communicate sufficiently about the reasons for their actions? But in the end, quietly and secretly, Socrates laughed at himself as well. He found the same difficulty and inability in himself when he examined himself before his more subtle conscience. But why, he persuaded himself, why give up the instincts on that account? It is necessary to do justice both to them *and* to reason; one must follow one's instincts and persuade rationality to help them out by giving them good reasons for being. This was the essential *falseness* of that great, mysterious ironist. He educated his conscience to be satisfied with a sort of self-deception. Basically he had seen through irrationality in moral judgments. Plato, who was more innocent about such things and who did not possess the plebeian's shrewdness, wanted, with the expenditure of all his strength—the greatest strength that any philosopher heretofore had at his disposal—to prove to himself that instinct and reason have the same natural aim, that both aim at the good, at "God." And all the theologians and philosophers since Plato have been on the same track. Which is to say that instinct, or "faith," as the Christians say, or "herd" as I say, has been victorious in the field of morality. One might except Descartes, the father of rationalism (hence grandfather of the Revolution), who acknowledged only the authority of reason. However his reason was only an instrument and Descartes was superficial.

### 192.

Whoever has pursued the history of any single science finds in its development a clue for the understanding of the most ancient and common processes of all "knowing and cognizing." There as here, the premature hypotheses, the fictitious creations, the good stupid will to "believe," the lack of suspiciousness and patience, are developed first. Our senses learn late, and never wholly, to be subtle, faithful, and cautious organs of cognition. It feels more comfortable to our eyes to reproduce upon a given stimulus an image already produced than to retain what is different and new in a given impression; the latter process requires more energy, more "morality," To hear something new is painful and difficult for the ear; we hear new music poorly. When we hear a foreign language we try unconsciously to re-form the sounds into words that sound more familiar and home-like. Thus, for example, the Germans fixed up for themselves the word *Armbrust* (arm-breast) when they heard *arcubalista* (cross-bow). Everything new finds even our senses hostile and unwilling, and more than unwilling. The passions like fear, love, and hatred (including the passive passions like laziness) *rule* the "simplest" processes of our sense activity. As little as a modern reader reads the individual words (not to mention syllables) on a page, but out of every twenty words takes perhaps five at random and "guesses" the presumable sense that goes with these five, so little do we see a tree exactly and completely as to its leaves, branches, colors, and forms. It is so much easier to imagine an approximation of a tree. Even in the midst of our most notable experiences we do the same thing. We invent the largest part of the thing experienced and can hardly be compelled *not* to observe some process with the eyes of an "inventor." All of this wants to say that we are basically and from time immemorial *accustomed to lying*. Or, to say it more virtuously and slyly, hence pleasantly: we are much greater artists than we know.—In the course of an animated conversation I often see the face of my partner, depending on the thought he has uttered or that I think I have evoked, so significantly and subtly defined that the degree of significance surpasses by far my visual capabilities. The subtlety of the play of muscles and the expression of the eyes that I "saw" *must* have been fictitiously created by me. In all probability the person made an entirely different face, or none at all.

### 193.

*Quidquid luce fuit, tenebris agit,*[3] but the opposite is also true! What we experience in dreams, assuming that we experience it frequently, belongs in the end as much to the total economy of our psyche as any "real" experience. We are richer or poorer by it, have one need more or less, and are finally guided somewhat by the habits of our dreams in bright, broad daylight and during the gayest and serenest moments of our waking thoughts. If, for example, someone has often flown in his dreams, and in the end is conscious, as soon as he dreams, of his power and skill in flying as though he enjoyed a special privilege and possessed a happiness most enviably his own—how should such a person, who thinks he can realize every sort of swoop and curve with his faintest impulse, who knows the feeling of a

[3] Whatever is started in the light continues in the dark.

divine levity, an "upward" without tension or compulsion, a "downward" without condescension or humiliation, without *gravity*—how should a person of such dream-experiences and dream-habits not find the word "happiness" to be of another color and definition during his waking periods as well! How should he not demand a *different* type of happiness! "Uplift" as described by the poets must seem too earth-bound, too muscular and violent, too "grave" to him, as compared with the "flying" of his dreams.

## 194.

The difference between people shows up not only in the difference between their value tables, in the fact, in other words, that they consider different goods most worth striving for and also that they disagree over the larger or smaller value, the order of rank, of their commonly acknowledged goods— the difference between people shows up even more in what they consider to be a real *having* or *possessing* of a good. With reference to a woman, for example, a modest man is satisfied if her body and her sex are at his disposal; this is a sufficient and satisfactory token of his having, his possessing her. Another man, with a more suspicious and demanding thirst for possession, sees the "question mark," the illusory quality of such having and demands more subtle tests; above all, he must know whether the woman not merely gives herself to him but whether for his sake she gives up other things that she likes or might like—only in *this* way does he consider her "possessed." A third man, however, has even here not reached the end of his distrust and desire to own;

he asks himself if the woman who gives up all else for him does not do so merely for a phantom of him; he wants first to be thoroughly, abysmally known by her before he can let himself be loved; he dares to be intuited. He does not feel the beloved to be wholly in his possession until she no longer deceives herself about him, until she loves him for his devilishness and concealed insatiability as much as for his goodness, patience, and spirituality.— Still another man wants to possess a whole people, and all the superior Cagliostro- and Catilina-tricks suit him for this purpose. Another, with a more subtle thirst for possession, tells himself that one must not deceive where one wishes to possess. He becomes irritated and impatient with the idea that a mask of him is ruling the people's heart, hence "I must *allow* myself to be known for what I am and first of all must know myself!" Among helpful and charitable people one finds almost regularly that awkward guile which first fixes up the person to be helped, until he suits their own purpose. They say, for example, that he "deserves" help, or that he demands *their* help and none other, or that he will prove to be deeply grateful, affectionate, and sub- missive when he has received their help. With such imaginings they control the needy as though they were a property of theirs. In fact, of course, they are helpful and charitable to begin with because of their demand for personal property of this sort. One finds them jealous if one crosses them or anticipates them when they are being helpful. Parents involuntarily do something similar to their children. They call it "bringing them up right." Basically, no mother doubts at the bottom of her heart that she has borne a property for herself; no father yields the right to submit the child to *his* concepts and valuations. It used to be, in fact, that fathers assumed the right to decide upon the life or death of their newborn (among the ancient Germanic tribes, for example). And, like the fathers, so nowadays the teachers, the professions, the priests, and the kings. In every man who comes under their control they see an unquestionable opportunity to add to their possessions. From which follows. . . .

### 195.

The Jews: a people "born for slavery" say Tacitus and the whole ancient world, "the chosen people among the peoples of the world," they themselves say and believe. The Jews have managed that miraculous reversal of values that produced a new and dangerous fascination for life on earth for a couple of millenniums. Their prophets melted down into one notion the notions "rich," "godless," "violent," and "sensual" and coined for the first time the shameful meaning of the word "world." In this reversal of the values (another part of it is the use of "poor" as synonymous with "holy" and "friend") lies the significance of the Jewish people: here is the beginning of the *slave revolt in morality*.

### 196.

There are countless dark bodies which must be *inferred* to lie near the sun; we shall never be able to see them. Among ourselves, that is a parable: a moral psychologist reads the whole language of the stars as only an allegorical and symbolic language. Many things can be kept dark with it.

### 197.

We thoroughly misunderstand the beast of prey and the man of prey (Cesare Borgia, for example); we thoroughly misunderstand "nature" as long as we seek a "diseased condition" at the bottom of these healthiest of all tropical monsters and growths. Or, even worse, as long as we seek an inborn "hell" in them, as almost all moralists have heretofore done. It seems, doesn't it, that moralists have a hatred for the primeval forests and the tropics. And that "tropical man" must be discredited at any cost, either as a diseased and degenerated form of mankind, or else as his own hell and self-torture. But why? In favor of the "temperate zones"? In favor of "temperate men"? Of "moral men"? Of mediocre men?—This much as contribution to the chapter, "Morality as timidity."

### 198.

All these moralities that address themselves to the individual, to make him "happy," as they say, what else are they but suggestions for the individual's behavior in relation to the degree of *dangerousness* in which he lives with himself. They are recipes against his passions, his good and wicked inclinations insofar as they have a will to power and would like to dominate. They are small and great shrewdnesses and artifices to which clings a stuffy odor of old home remedies and old-wives' wisdoms; all these moralities are baroque in form and devoid of sense because they address themselves to everyone, because they generalize where there can be no generalization. They all talk absolutes, take themselves to be absolutes; they must be seasoned with more than a grain of salt. They only become endurable, in fact (and possibly quite enticing), when they are over-seasoned and learn to smell of danger, above all of "the other world." All this, by intellectual standards, is not worth much and certainly is not "science," not to speak of "wisdom." Let me repeat it three times: it is shrewdness, shrewdness, shrewdness, mixed with stupidity, stupidity, stupidity, whether it be the in-difference and statue-like coldness toward the heated foolishness of the passions that the Stoics prescribed and attempted to cure with, or whether it be that "never laugh again and never weep again" recipe of Spinoza, his so naïvely recommended destruction of the passions through analyzing and vivisecting them; or that toning down of the passions till they reach a harmless mediocrity with which they are to be satisfied—moral Aristotelianism; or even morality in the form of enjoyment of the passions, but in an intentional adulteration and spiritualization, as can be found in the symbolism of art or in music or in the love for God or in the love for mankind for God's sake (for the passions are allowed citizen's rights in the form of religion, provided they. . . .); or finally whether it be that obliging and spirited surrender to the passions that Hafis and Goethe taught, that bold dropping of the reins, that spiritual-physical *licentia morum,* but only in the exceptional case of old codgers and drunks who will hardly any longer "get into trouble." This, too, for the chapter, "Morality as timidity."

## 199.

Since at all times, as long as there have been human beings, there have been human herds (clan unions, communities, tribes, nations, states, churches) and very many who obeyed compared with very few who were in command; since, therefore, obedience was the trait best and longest exercised and cultivated among men, one may be justified in assuming that on the average it has become an innate need, a kind of *formal conscience* that bids "thou shalt do something or other absolutely, and absolutely refrain from something or other," in other words, "thou shalt." This need seeks to satisfy itself and to fill its form with some content. Depending on how strong, impatient, and tense it is, it seizes upon things with little discrimination, like a gross appetite, and accepts whatever meets its ear, whatever any representative of authority (parents, teachers, laws, class prejudices, public opinion) declaims into it. The strange limitation of human evolution, the factors that make for hesitation, protractedness, retrogression, and circular paths, is due to the fact that the herd-instinct of obedience is best inherited at the expense of knowing how to command. Let us imagine this instinct taking over to its limits: in the end there would be none whatever who could command or be independent; or else all those in command would in the end suffer inwardly from a bad conscience and have to practice a self-deception before they could command, namely pretend that they too are only obeying. This is in fact what is true of Europe today: the moral hypocrisy, as I call it, of those in command. They know of no means of protection against their bad conscience except to posture as executors of older or higher commands (ancestors, constitutions, justice, the law, or even God). They even borrow herd-maxims from the herd's way of thinking, such as "the people's serv-

ant" or "instruments of the common good." The
herd-man, on the other side, pretends today in
Europe that he is the only permissible type of man;
he glorifies the qualities which make him tame,
agreeable, and useful to the rest of the herd, as *the*
human virtues: social conscience, good intentions,
consideration, diligence, moderation, unpretentious-
ness, tolerance, compassion. For those cases, however, where one believes one needs leaders and bell-
wethers, one attempts today again and again to replace commanders with a pooling of clever herd-
men: all the European constitutions owe their origin
to such an attempt. That the appearance of an absolute commander for these herd-Europeans, in spite
of everything, is a deed of kindness, a relief from
steadily more unendurable pressure, was last attested
in the grand manner by the rise of Napoleon. The
history of Napoleon's effectiveness is almost the
history of the higher happiness which this whole
century attained in its most valuable men and moments.

## 200.

The human being who stems from an age of dissolution that shuffles and rearranges the races, who has
the heritage of manifold origins in his body (which is
to say antithetical and sometimes not even antithetical instincts and standards of value that fight each
other and rarely come to rest)—such a man of a late
culture and refracted lights will on the average be
a rather weak man. His innermost desire is that the
war which he *is* should come to an end; happiness
seems to him (and the Epicurean and Christian
sedatives he gets help this belief) to be primarily the
bliss of resting, of remaining undisturbed, of satiety,

of final at-one-ness, as the "sabbath of sabbaths" to speak with that holy rhetorician St. Augustine who was himself such a man.—But if the antitheses and warlikeness of such a nature have the effect of being one *more* impulse and challenge to life, and if, on the other hand, the craftsmanship and subtlety necessary for war have been inherited and developed along with the powerful and irreconcilable instincts—if, in other words, such a person is capable of controlling and outwitting himself, then we get one of those enchantingly impalpable and unimaginable human riddles, predestined for victory and seduction, whose loveliest representatives were Alcibiades and Caesar (I should like to add, so far as my own taste is concerned, that *first* European, Frederick II of Hohenstaufen) and, among artists, perhaps Leonardo da Vinci. They appear precisely at the time when the weaker type with its demand for peacefulness becomes noticeable. Both types belong together and spring from the same causes.

### 201.

As long as the principle of utility that rules moral value judgments is only utility for the herd, as long as the outlook is directed solely at the preservation of the social community and immorality is sought exactly and exclusively in whatever seems dangerous to the status quo—there can be no "morality of neighborly love." Agreed that even then there is some constant minor exercise of consideration, compassion, fairness, gentleness, and mutual helpfulness, agreed that even in this state of society all the impulses are active that will later be honored as "virtues" and finally coincide, practically speaking, with the very concept of morality—nonetheless, in the period of which we speak, they do not yet belong in the realm of moral values; they are still *amoral*. A compassionate deed during the best period of Rome, for example, was labelled neither good nor evil, neither moral nor immoral. If it was praised, a sort of reluctant disdain was not at all incompatible with the praise—as soon as the deed was compared to an act which served the furtherance of the whole, the *res publica*. Ultimately, love for one's neighbor is always something subsidiary, partly conventional and arbitrarily manifested, when compared with *fear of one's neighbor*. After the social structure as a whole is stabilized and secured against external dangers, it is the fear of one's neighbor that creates new perspectives of moral valuations. Certain strong and dangerous drives, such as love for enterprise, foolhardiness, revenge, cunning, rapacity, and love for domination, all of them traits that had just been not only honored as being socially useful (under other names than these, as seems fair enough), but actually cultivated and fostered (because they were constantly needed to overcome the common danger imposed by the common enemy)—now, with the outlet channels gone, are gradually branded as immoral and given over to defamation. Now the antithetical drives and inclinations come into their own so far as morality is concerned. The herd-instinct draws its conclusions, step by step. How much or how little the common good is endangered, the dangers to the status quo that lie in a given opinion, or state, or passion, in a given will or talent—these now furnish the moral perspective. Here too fear is once again the mother of morality. Communal solidarity is annihilated by the highest and strongest drives that, when they break out passionately, whip the individual far past the average low level of the herd-conscience; society's belief in itself, its backbone as it were, breaks. Hence such drives will best be branded and defamed. A superior, independent intellect, a will to stand alone, even a superior rationality, are felt to be dangers; everything that lifts the individual above the herd and causes fear in his neighbor is from now on called *evil;* the fair-minded, unassuming disposition that adapts and equalizes, all mediocrity of desires comes to be called and honored by the name of morality. Finally, when conditions are very peaceful, all opportunity and necessity for cultivating one's feelings for rigor and hardness disappear; now any rigor, even in the operations of justice, begins to disturb men's conscience. Any superior and rigorous distinction and self-responsibility is felt to be almost insulting; it awakens mistrust; the "lambs" and even more the "sheep" gain respect. There is a point of pathological hollowness and over-indulgence in the history of social groups where they even side with those who harm them, with their criminals—and they feel this way seriously and honestly. Punishment seems somehow unfair; at any rate it is certain that the idea of punishment, of having to punish, hurts the group. It creates fear in them. "Isn't it enough to render him *harmless?* Why punish on top of that? Punishment itself is frightful!" With this sentiment the morality of timidity, the herd-morality, draws its ultimate conclusion. If one could abolish danger, abolish the grounds for fear, one would have abolished this morality along with it; it would no longer be necessary; it would no longer consider *itself* necessary! Anyone who tests the conscience of today's European, will pull the same imperative out of a thousand moral folds and hiding places, the imperative of herd-timidity: "We desire that someday there shall be *nothing more to fear.*" Someday—the will and way to that someday is everywhere in Europe today called "progress."

## 202.

Let us immediately say once again what we have said a hundred times already, for today's ears are not good-naturedly open to such truths—to any of *our* truths. We know very well how insulting it sounds when someone counts man among the animals, without further ado and without allegory; but they will almost consider us *guilty* for constantly talking about the man of "modern ideas" in terms of "herd" and "herd-instinct" and such. How can it be helped! We cannot do otherwise, for this precisely is the point of our new insight. We found that so far as all the major moral judgments are concerned, Europe is today of one mind (including the countries that are affected by European influence): Europe obviously *knows* today what Socrates thought he did not know and what that famous old serpent promised to teach —they "know" today what is good and what is evil. Now of course it sounds harsh and hard on the ears when we keep insisting that whatever believes it knows, whatever glorifies itself with its praise and blame, whatever approves of itself, is the instinct of the human herd-animal, the instinct which has broken out, is more and more preponderating, more and more dominating the other instincts, in accordance with the growing physiological approximation and resemblance of which it is the symptom. *Morality in Europe today is herd-animal morality,* that is—as we understand things—*one type* of human morality, beside which and before and after which many other moralities, above all, more superior moralities, are possible or *should* be possible. But against such a possibility and against such a "should" this morality defends itself with all its might; stubbornly and inexorably it says, "I myself am morality itself and nothing other than myself is morality!" With the aid of a religion, in fact, which agreed with and flattered the most sublime desires of herd-animals, we have come to the point where even in the political and social institutions an increasingly visible expression of this morality can be found: the *democratic* movement comes into the Christian inheritance. But that the democratic tempo is much too slow and sleepy for the impatient ones, the sick sufferers from the above mentioned instinct, is attested by the ever more raging howls, the ever more open baring of the teeth of the anarchist-dogs who are now flitting through the alleys of European culture. They are seemingly opposed to the peaceable and hard-working democrats, to the ideological revolutionaries, and even more to the bungling philosophasters and brotherhood-visionaries who call themselves Socialists and desire a "free society"—but in actuality the anarchists are of the same breed, of the same thorough and instinctive hostility against any social structure other than that of the *autonomous* herd (they go so far as to reject the concepts "master" and "servant"—*ni dieu ni maître* is one of the Socialist slogans); they are one with all the others in their tough resistance against any special claim, any special privilege and special right (basically this means they are against all rights, for when all are equal no one needs any more "rights"); they are one in their distrust of punitive justice (as though it were a violation of the weaker, a wrong against the *necessary* succession of all earlier forms of society); they are one in their religion of compassion, of fellow-feeling that extends to every feeling, living, suffering thing (down to the animal and up as far as "God": the extravagance of "compassion for God" belongs to a democratic age); they are one in the shriek, the impatience, of their compassion; one in deathly hatred against suffering as such, in their almost feminine inability to remain spectators at suffering, to *allow* suffering to take place; they are one in the involuntary depression and molly-coddling under whose spell Europe seems threatened by a new form of Buddhism; they are one in their faith in the morality of *commonly felt* compassion as though this feeling constituted morality itself, as though it were the summit, the *attained* summit of mankind, the only hope of the future, the consolation of the living, the great deliverance from all the guilt of yore—they are all one in their faith in fellowship as that which will *deliver* them, their faith in the herd, in other words, in "themselves". . . .

### 203.

We, who are of a different faith, for whom the democratic movement is not only a deteriorated form of political organization but a deterioration, that is to say, a depreciation of a human type, a mediocritizing and lowering of values—where must our hopes look? We have no other choice: we must seek *new philosophers,* spirits strong or original enough to give an impulse to opposing valuations, to transvalue and turn upside down the "eternal values"; we must seek heralds, men of the future, who will now tie the knot and start the pressure that shall force the will of millenniums to run *new* orbits. Men who will teach man that man's future is man's *will,*

dependent on man's will; who will prepare great
ventures and all-involving experiments of discipline
and culture so that there will be an end to that gruesome rule of nonsense and accident that is called
"history" (the nonsense of the "greatest number" is
merely its last manifestation). For such tasks we
shall some day require a new type of philosopher and
commander, compared with whom any previous concealed, frightful, or well-intentioned spirits will seem
pale and dwarfish. The image of such leaders is what
hovers before *our* eyes. May I say it aloud, you free
thinkers? The conditions one would have to partly
create, partly utilize, for their development, the presumable paths and tests by which a soul could grow
to such height and might, by which it could learn to
feel the *compulsion* to such tasks, a transvaluation of
values beneath whose new pressure and hammer a
conscience is forged, a heart is transformed into
bronze, so that it might bear the weight of such a
responsibility; furthermore the necessity for such
leaders, the horrifying danger that they might fail to
appear, or turn out wrong or degenerate—all these
are *our* essential cares and depressions. You free
thinkers know it is so. These are the grave distant
thoughts, the thunderclouds that pass over the skies
of *our* lives. There are few pains as keen as to have
seen, guessed and felt how some extraordinary man
has degenerated and falls out of his orbit. But whoever has that rare eye for the universal danger, the
danger that mankind itself might deteriorate; whoever like us has once recognized the monstrous ran-
domness which hitherto has played its game with the
future of man, a game in which no hand, not even a
"finger of God" has ever taken part; whoever intuits
the doom that lies hidden in the idiotic guilelessness

and blind self-confidence of "modern ideas," even
more of all Christian-European morality—such a
man suffers an anxiety with which none other can be
compared. For he comprehends with a glance what
all *could be cultivated in mankind* if there were a
favorable accumulation and heightening of powers
and tasks; he knows with all the science of his conscience how unexhausted man still is for his greatest
possibilities, and how often the type "mankind" has
faced mysterious decisions and new paths; he knows
even better through his most painful recollections
that wretched things usually have caused some development of the highest potential rank to break
apart, break off, sink back, become wretched. *The
universal degeneration of mankind* down to what the
Socialist bunglers and flatheads today call the "man
of the future," down to their ideal, the degeneration
and depreciation of man until he is a perfect herd
animal (or, to use their words, "man in a free society"), this brutalization of man until he is a
dwarfed beast with equal rights and equal demands
—this is *possible*. There can be no doubt about it.
Whoever has fully thought out this possibility has
one more nausea than the others—and also, perhaps,
a new *task*.—

# SIXTH ARTICLE

## WE INTELLECTUALS

### 204.

At the risk that moralizing here as elsewhere will show up as what Balzac called a resolute *montrer ses plaies*,[1] I should nonetheless like to venture an opposition to that improper and harmful confusion as to rank which threatens to arise today, quite unnoted and apparently with the best conscience, in the fields of science[2] and of philosophy. It seems to me that someone who has had experience in science (and experience always seems to imply bad experience!), someone with scientific training, should have the right to enter upon a discussion which treats of rather subtle problems of rank. For it will not do to talk about science like a blind man about color. Such talk is reserved for women and artists whose instinct and modesty always sighs, "Alas, that terrible science, it always gets to the *bottom!*"—The declaration of independence of the scientific man, his emancipation from philosophy, is one of the most subtle after-effects of the democratic nature and unnaturalness; the self-glorification and conceit of the intellectual stands today in full bloom and in its best spring-time —although one could hardly say that self-praise in this case smelled sweet.[3] "Freedom from all masters,"

[1] Showing one's wounds.

[2] By science (German: *Wissenschaft*) Nietzsche means the learned disciplines, including not only the natural and social sciences but what are known in this country as the humanities. *Translator.*

[3] Nietzsche alludes to the German proverb, "Self-praise stinks." *Translator.*

here too is the instinct of rabble, and after science successfully fought off theology whose handmaiden it was for so long, it is now prepared, with complete recklessness and lack of understanding, to legislate for philosophy and to play "master" to it, for a change. Worse than that, science wants to play the *philosopher*. My memory (the memory of a scientifically trained man, if you will allow me)[4] is stuffed with the naïvetés of conceit that I have heard from young natural scientists and from old physicians who have talked about philosophy and philosophers—not to mention the most cultured and most conceited of all intellectuals, the philologists and academics who need both culture and conceit to qualify for their profession. Sometimes it was the specialist and little-jack-horner who defended himself instinctively against all non-analytic tasks and capabilities; at other times it was the diligent scientific worker who got a smell of *otium* and of the whole distinguished luxury that furnishes the psychic household of the philosopher, and felt himself encroached upon or belittled by it. Then again it was the color blindness of the Utilitarian who sees nothing in philosophy except a series of *refuted* systems and a wasteful extravagance which "does no one any good." Sometimes it was the fear of disguised mysticism and the boundary-adjustments of cognition that broke forth, then again it was a low opinion of certain philosophers that was involuntarily generalized into a low opinion of all philosophy. But most frequently I found behind the

---

[4] Nietzsche received his training at the universities of Bonn and Leipzig in classical philology. From 1869-79 he was Professor of Classical Philology at the University of Basel in Switzerland. At the age of 35 he resigned from this job, receiving a university pension which kept him alive, to write his major works. He travelled almost constantly between Switzerland and Italy, visiting Germany only at rare intervals. *Translator.*

arrogant disdain of philosophy that young intellectuals profess, the ill-after-effects of some individual philosopher, someone whom they had given up without having been able to shed his scornful valuation of other philosophers. And this produced ill will toward philosophy generally. (This, for example, seems to me to characterize Schopenhauer's influence on the present generation; with his unintelligent rage against Hegel he has managed to break a whole generation of Germans loose from their connections with German culture, a culture which, everything considered, consisted of a superior, intuitive refinement of the *historical sense*. Schopenhauer himself, of course, was poor, unreceptive, and un-German in this respect, to the point of genius!) In any event, speaking generally, it was probably the human, all-too-human aspect, the wretchedness of recent philosophers, that spoiled most radically people's reverence for philosophy and opened the gates to the plebeian instincts. Why don't we admit the degree to which our modern world lacks the type of Heraclites, Plato, Empedocles and whoever else were the regal and magnificent anchorites of the spirit! Why don't we admit that a decent man of science *should* feel superior as to type and breeding to such representatives of philosophy who, thanks to fashion, are today both at the top and down and out—in Germany the two Lions of Berlin, for example, the anarchist Eugen Dühring and the amalgamist Eduard von Hartmann! In particular, it is the sight of the hodge-podge philosophers who call themselves "reality philosophers" or "Positivists" that can cause a dangerous distrust in the soul of a young ambitious intellectual. He must tell himself that, at best, they too are intellectuals and learned specialists (as is painfully obvious!);

they have all been overwhelmed; they have *returned* to the service of science after having demanded more of themselves and having found that they had no right to this "more" and its attendant responsibilities. And now they represent in word and deed, sincerely, grimly, and vengefully, the *disbelief* that philosophy is a lordly task and a form of ruling. And ultimately, how could they believe otherwise! Science today is in flower, with a clear conscience shining from its face, while that to which modern philosophy has gradually dwindled, the remains of current philosophical opinion, excites distrust and displeasure if not scorn and compassion. Philosophy reduced to theory of knowledge, actually no more than a bashful "periodism" and doctrine of continence—a philosophy which cannot get past its own threshold and has painstakingly *forbidden* its own right to enter—this surely is philosophy in its last throes, an end, an agony, something that arouses compassion. How could such a philosophy *rule*?

### 205.

The dangers to the development of a philosopher are truly so manifold today, that one may well doubt if such fruit can still ripen. The extent and height of the sciences has grown to be enormous; hence also the probability that a philosopher will grow fatigued while he is still learning, and will permit himself to be attached somewhere and become specialized. This means, of course, that he will never reach his own potential height, hence that he will never get an overall view, a view of the whole, a view *from the top down*. Or else he will get to the top too late; he will get there when his best time and power are over, or so injured, coarsened, and deteriorated, that his view, his total value judgment, signifies little. Precisely the subtlety of his intellectual conscience may make him hesitate and tarry on the way; he fears the temptation to become a dilettante, or else a millepede or a milleantenna; he knows all too well that someone who has lost reverence for himself no longer commands, even so far as cognition is concerned. He no longer *leads*, not, at least, unless he becomes a great actor, a philosophic Cagliostro or Pied Piper, i.e. a seducer. In the end it becomes a question of taste, even if it were not a question of conscience. Add to this, to double the philosopher's difficulties, that he demands of himself a judgment, a Yes and No, not as to some science, but as to life and life's worth. But he dislikes learning to believe that he has the right or, worse yet, the duty to make such a judgment; only from his most extensive, perhaps most disturbing and destructive experiences can he search out his way to that right, that belief. Often he will search hesitantly, doubtfully, and increasingly silently. The masses have mistaken and misrecognized the philosopher for a long time in fact; sometimes they took him for a scientific man and an ideal intellectual; sometimes for a religiously-elevated, "demoralized," "unworldly" enthusiast—a divine alcoholic, as it were. If by any chance one hears praise today for someone who lives "wisely" or "philosophically," it amounts to hardly more than "shrewdly and passively." Wisdom to the rabble is a sort of escape, a trick for withdrawing successfully from an outrageous game. But for *us,* my friends, the philosopher lives "unphilosophically" and "unwisely" and above all un-shrewdly. He feels the burden and duty to take up the hundreds of experiments and temptations of life; he constantly risks *himself;* he plays the outrageous game. . . .

## 206.

In relation to a genius, a creature, that is to say, who either *impregnates* or *gives birth*—taking both expressions in their fullest sense—the intellectual, the average man of science, has something of the old maid about him. Like the old maid, he does not understand the two most valuable functions of mankind. To both, as a matter of fact, to both the intellectual and the old maid we concede a kind of respectability, by way of compensating their deficiency. The respectability is emphasized, and a double amount of vexation is due to the fact that we are forced to such a concession. Let us look more closely: what is the scientific man? First of all, he is an undistinguished type of man, with the virtues of an undistinguished, i.e. non-ruling, non-authoritative, and non-self-sufficient type. He is hard-working, a patient rank and filer, equable and limited as to abilities and requirements. He has an instinct for others like himself and for what is good for him and them: that bit of independence and green pasture, for example, without which no work can be done in peace; that claim to honor and recognition (which above all assumes recognizability); that sunshine of a good reputation; that constant ratification of his worth and his usefulness which must again and again overcome the inward distrust, the heart's core, of all dependent men and herd-animals. The intellectual has, as one might expect, the diseases and the naughtinesses of an undistinguished type: he is full of petty envy; he has lynx eyes for the pettiness of those natures whose heights he cannot share. He is friendly, but only like someone who can let himself go, but not *flow:* faced with men of great flow, he stands all the more cold and unreceptive—his eyes like a smooth, unwilling sea, ruffled by no delight, no response. The worst and most dangerous thing of which the intellectual is capable stems from the mediocrity of his type: from that Jesuitical mediocrity which instinctively labors to destroy any unusual man; which seeks to break every tight-drawn bow, or better yet, to slacken it. For slackening (considerately, with a kind, guiding hand, to be sure), slackening full of friendly compassion: this is the essential skill of Jesuitism which has always known enough to introduce itself as the religion of compassion.

## 207.

However gratefully we may meet the spirit of objectivity half-way (and who hasn't been sick to death of everything subjective and its damned *ipsissimosity!*)—in the end we must learn to be cautious even with our gratitude and to take steps against the exaggeration with which the self-stripping and depersonalization of the mind as an end in itself is currently celebrated, as a means of redemption and transfiguration. This happens particularly within the school of Pessimism which, to be sure, has good reason to accord the highest honors to "disinterested cognition." An objective man who no longer curses and scolds as the Pessimist does, the *ideal* intellectual in whom the scientific instinct after thousands of semi- and total failures for once comes to bloom and fruition, is surely one of the most precious instruments in the world. But he belongs in the hands of one who has greater power. He is only an instrument

—he is a *mirror,* let us say; he is not an "end in himself." The objective man is indeed a mirror; above all he is something that wishes to be recognized and understood; he is accustomed to subordination, devoid of any pleasure other than that afforded by cognition, by "mirroring." He waits until something comes along and then spreads himself out delicately, so that even faint footprints and the slipping by of ghostly creatures shall not be lost to his surface, to his sensitive hide. Whatever "person" is left in him seems accidental to him, often arbitrary, even more often disturbing. To such an extent he has become the passageway and reflection for other figures and events in his own estimation. Only with an effort does he recall "himself," and often he recalls himself erroneously; he easily mixes himself up with others; he makes the wrong decision in regard to his own basic needs. In this respect alone he is un-subtle and careless. Perhaps he is plagued by his own state of health or the pettiness and sticky atmosphere of his wife and friends, or the lack of fellowship and society. He will force himself to reflect on his tortures, but in vain. His thought instantly wanders away from himself, to a *more general* instance, and tomorrow he will know as little about what he needs as he does today. He has lost the ability and the time to take himself seriously; he is serene, not from lack of troubles, but from lack of skill in handling *his* troubles. His habit of meeting everything and every experience half way, the sunny and unembarrassed hospitality with which he accepts all comers, his type of unthinking good-naturedness, his dangerous indifference as to Yes and No: alas, there are enough instances in which he has to atone for these virtues of his; as a human being generally, he all too easily

becomes the *caput mortuum*[5] of his virtues. If one
asks love or hate of him—and I mean love or hate
as God, women, and animals understand them—well,
he will do what he can and give what he can. But
no one should be surprised when it turns out not to
be much, when in this respect he shows up false,
fragile, questionable, and hollow. His love is over-
intentional; his hate is artificial and really a *tour
de force,* a small vanity and exaggeration. We must
accept that he is only genuine insofar as he is permitted to be objective; it is only in his serene
"totalism" that he is a part of nature and acts
"natural." His mirroring and forever smoothing
soul no longer knows how to affirm or deny; he does
not command; neither does he destroy. He agrees
with Leibniz: *"Je ne méprise presque rien"*[6]—and
we must not fail to hear or underrate the *presque.*
He is not a model man, either; he walks neither before nor behind anyone; he places himself at too
remote a point to side with either good or evil.
Insofar as we have long mistaken him for a *philosopher,* for the Caesar-like disciplinarian and forcer
of culture, we have honored him far too highly
and have overlooked his essential nature. He is
an instrument, a piece of slave—the most sublime
type of slave, to be sure, but in himself: *presque
rien.* The objective man is an instrument, a precious,
easily injured, easily clouded instrument for taking
measurements. As a mirror he is a work of art, to
be handled carefully and honored. But he is not
an aim, not a way out nor a way up, not a comple-
mentary human being through whom the *rest* of
existence is justified, not a conclusion. And still

[5] Dry residue.
[6] I despise scarcely anything.

less is he a beginning, an impregnation, or a first
cause; he is nothing solid, nothing powerful, nothing
self-reliant seeking to become master. Rather, a delicate, hollow, subtle, and mobile potter's form that
must wait for some content, some substance, in
order to be shaped accordingly; he is usually a man
without substance or content, a "self-less" man.
Hence, not a man for women, either (parenthetically
remarked)—

## 208.

When a philosopher makes it known today that he
is not a skeptic (I trust that this has been gathered
from the above description of the objective spirit),
no one likes to hear him. Everyone looks at him
with some embarrassment; they would like to ask
so many, many questions. Among a timid audience,
in fact (and there are many of them today), he is
henceforth known as dangerous. It seems to them,
when they hear him reject skepticism, that they can
dimly hear in the distance an evil threatening noise,
as though a new explosive were being tested, a dyna-
mite of the spirit, perhaps a newly invented Russian
*nihiline,* a Pessimism of good will which does not
merely say "no" or want "no" but—horrible thought
—will *do* "no." Against such a type of "good will,"
the will to a real, active negation of life, there is no
better-known or more successful soporific or sedative
today than skepticism, the gentle, sweet, lulling
poppy-juice called skepticism. Hamlet himself is today prescribed by the doctors of the hour to cure
"mind" and its underground rumblings. "Aren't
our ears already deafened by all sorts of wicked
noises?" says the skeptic, the friend of peace and
quiet, the security-policeman. "This subterranean

'no' is frightful! Be quiet, now, you pessimistic moles!" For the skeptic, the delicate creature, is too easily shocked; his conscience has been trained to jump at every "no"—in fact even at a decisive, rigorous "yes"—and to feel as though it were being bitten. "Yes" and "no" run counter to his morality; on the other hand, he loves holding a banquet of noble continence for his virtues. He loves to say, with Montaigne, "What do I know?" Or, with Socrates, "I know that I know nothing." Or "I do not trust myself here; there is no door open for me here." Or "If a door were open, why enter?" Or "What is the use of hasty hypotheses? To assume no hypotheses whatever might easily be a mark of good taste. Why must you make everything crooked straight as fast as possible? Why stuff every hole with some kind of oakum? Isn't there enough time later? Doesn't time have lots of time? Oh you devils, can't you *wait?* Uncertainty too has its charms. The Sphinx too is a Circe, and Circe too was a philosophress!" Such are the consolations of a skeptic and it is true enough that he needs some consolation. For skepticism is the spiritual expression of a certain, varied physiological quality which in common language is called nervous weakness or sickliness. It arises every time long separated races or classes are crossed in a decisive and sudden way. Everything is restiveness, doubt, experimentation in the resultant new generation whose blood inherits, as it were, different standards and different values. The best of their powers have a blocking effect on one another; even their virtues do not let one another grow and become strong; balance, ballast, and perpendicular stability are lacking in body and soul. But it is the *will* that is most deeply sick and degenerated in such cross-breeds; they no longer know independence of decision, or the courageous pleasure that lies in willing; they doubt the "freedom of the will" even in their dreams. Our Europe of today, the scene of a senselessly sudden experiment in class upheaval (and *hence* race upheaval), is for this reason skeptical in all its heights and depths. It exhibits now that mobile skepticism which jumps impatiently and greedily from one branch to the next, now the dull sort, like a cloud overloaded with question marks. And it is frequently sick to death of its will! Paralysis of the will: this is the cripple one finds squatting everywhere today! And how decked out he is! How seductively decked out! There are the most beautiful pomp-and-deception garments for this disease. But that most of what today is labelled "objectivity," "scientific spirit," *"l'art pour l'art,"* "pure will-less cognition" in the shop windows is only decked-out skepticism and paralysis of the will: this diagnosis of the European disease is one I can guarantee.—The disease of the will is spread unevenly over Europe. Where culture has been longest at home, it shows up most virulent and varied; it disappears to the degree to which the "barbarian" is still (or again) claiming his rights under the baggy garments of western civilization. In today's France therefore (a palpable conclusion!), the will is most gravely ill. And France, which has always been superbly skillful at reversing the fateful turns of its spirit into something charming and seductive, today really shows its cultural leadership over Europe. It is the very school and show window of all the charms of skepticism. The power to will— and to persist until a given will has been fulfilled— is somewhat stronger in Germany. And within

Germany it is stronger in the North than in the central regions. It is considerably stronger still in England, Spain and Corsica, bound up with the phlegm of the former, with the hard heads of the latter nations—not to mention Italy which is too young a nation to know what its will is and which must first prove that it knows how to will. But the power to will is strongest and most astonishing in that enormous land of the middle where Europe flows back into Asia: in Russia. There the power to will has been stored and accumulated for ages; there the will—uncertain whether it is a will of negation or of affirmation—lies threateningly in wait to be discharged (to borrow the favorite word of today's physicists). It would not require merely wars in India and complications in Asia for Europe to be unburdened of its greatest danger, but interior upheavals, the atomization of the empire into many small bodies, and above all the introduction of parliamentarian nonsense, including the compulsion for everyone to read his newspaper while eating his breakfast. I am not saying this because I wish it so; the contrary would be closer to my heart's desire. I mean such an increase of Russia's threat that Europe would have to make up its mind to become equally threatening, namely to fuse into *a single will*, by means of a new caste that ruled over all Europe, one long terrible will of its own that might set itself aims which only millenniums could fulfill, so that there might finally be an end to the long-drawn-out comedy of petty state-ism with its dynastic as well as democratic divergent wills. The time for petty politics is over; the twentieth century will bring with it the struggle for world-dominion, the *compulsion* to high politics.

### 209.

How far the new warlike age into which we Europeans are obviously entering might be favorable to the development of another, stronger type of skepticism, I should like to indicate for the time being with a mere parable, one which friends who know German history will readily understand. That impetuous enthusiast for handsome, tall grenadiers, that king of Prussia who brought into being a military and skeptical genius (and in so doing helped a new, recently victorious type of German to emerge), the questionable and insane father of Frederick the Great, had in one particular, at least, the knack and lucky touch (claw, one might say) of genius. He knew what was lacking in the Germany of his time, and he knew that what was lacking was a hundred times more worrisome and urgent than the lack of culture and of social forms. His dislike of young Frederick rose out of a deep, instinctive fear. *Men were lacking.* He suspected, to his bitter displeasure, that his own son was not man enough. Here he was wrong, but who in his place could have thought otherwise? He saw his son given up to atheism, to *esprit,* to the pleasurable hedonism of witty Frenchmen; he saw in the background the great vampire, the spider skepticism; he suspiciously foresaw the incurable misery of a heart that is no longer rigorous, toward good as well as toward evil, of a broken will that no longer commands, that no longer knows *how* to command. But meanwhile a more dangerous and rigorous new type of skepticism was growing in the son—who knows *how* much it owed precisely to hatred of his father and to the icy melancholy of a will forced into solitude? It was the skepticism of bold manliness, closely related to the genius for war and conquest. In the figure of the Great Frederick it made its first entrance into Germany. This type of skepticism despises and nonetheless takes over; it undermines but takes possession; it has no belief but is not lost through unbelief; it gives dangerous freedom to the intellect but holds the heart in strict bounds. It is the *German* form of skepticism which, in the form of a continued and intellectualized spirit of Frederick the Great, kept Europe for some time under the sway of the German mind and the critical and historical skepticism which characterized it. Thanks to the insuperably strong and tough masculine character of the great German philologists and critical historians (all of them, when properly examined, artists of destruction and dissolution as well), gradually, and in spite of all romanticism in music and philosophy, a *new* concept of the German mind was formulated, a mind in which the inclination to masculine skepticism was decisive, whether it appeared as fearlessness of gaze, or as courage and rigor of the dissecting hand, or as the tough will to dangerous voyages of discovery, to spiritual North Pole expeditions beneath barren and dangerous skies. With good reason do warm-blooded and superficial humanity-men cross themselves when they catch sight of this type of mind: *cet esprit fataliste, ironique, méphistophélique,* says Michelet, not without a shudder. But if one wishes to feel the full impact of the honor implied by this fear of the "man" in the German mind through whom Europe was awakened from its "dogmatic slumbers," one need only remember the former concept of German mind, the concept which the new skepticism had to overcome. It is not long ago that a masculinized female could allow her-

self the unbridled presumption of recommending the
Germans to the loving interest of other Europeans
on the grounds that they were gentle, tender-hearted,
weak-willed, poetic dunces. And let us finally come
to a deeper understanding of Napoleon's astonishment when he saw Goethe. It reveals what the
"German mind" for centuries had been taken for.
Napoleon's *"Voilà un homme!"* properly translated,
means, "Why, this is a *man!* I had expected only a
German!"—

## 210.

If we admit, then, that in the image of the philosophers of the future some trait leads us to wonder
whether they must not perhaps be skeptics in the
last suggested sense, still it would be only something
in them which could be so characterized, *not* they
themselves. With equal justice they might allow
themselves to be called critics; and surely they will
be experimenters. By the name with which I ventured to christen them, I expressly emphasized their
experimentation and their delight in experimentation.
Did I do this because, as critics in body and soul,
they will love to make use of experimentation in
a new, perhaps wider, perhaps more dangerous
sense? In their passion for new insight, must they
go farther in bold and painful experiments than the
emasculate and morbid taste of a democratic century
can approve?—Of one thing there is no doubt: these
future philosophers will be least able to dispense
with the serious and not unobjectionable qualities
that distinguish the critic from the skeptic. I mean
a sureness as to standards of value, a conscious em-
ployment of a single method, a wary courage, an
ability to stand alone and be responsible for them-

selves. In fact, among themselves they will admit to a certain pleasure in saying "no", in dissecting, and in a certain circumspect cruelty which knows how to handle the knife surely and delicately, even when the heart is bleeding. They will be *harder* (and perhaps not always only toward themselves) than humane people might wish; they will not go in for truth in order to be "pleased" or "elevated" or "inspired." On the contrary, they will have little faith that "truth" of all things should carry along such delights for the feelings. They will smile, these stern spirits, if any one should say in their presence, "This thought elevates me; how could it be untrue?" Or, "This work enchants me, how could it be unbeautiful?" Or, "That artist magnifies me, how could he be other than magnificent?" Perhaps they will have not merely a smile but a genuine disgust ready for everything thus rapturous, idealistic, effeminate, and hermaphroditic. And anyone looking into the secret chambers of their hearts would hardly find there an intention to reconcile "Christian sentiments" with "antique taste" or—worse—with "modern parliamentarism." (This is a kind of reconciliation which is reputedly found even among philosophers in our very uncertain and therefore very conciliatory century). Critical discipline, and every habit that leads to purity and rigor in matters of the spirit, will be demanded not only from themselves by these philosophers of the future. They may in fact wear them as a sort of jewel, for all to see. But they do not wish to be called critics on this account. It seems to them no small indignity to philosophy when it is decreed, as happens so readily today, "Philosophy itself is criticism and critical science—and nothing else besides." Let this evaluation of philosophy enjoy the applause of all the Positivists of France and Germany (it might even have flattered the heart and taste of Kant—let us remember the titles of his principal works!), our new philosophers will nonetheless say: Critics are instruments of the philosopher, and being instruments, are precisely for that reason far from being philosophers themselves! Even the great Chinaman of Koenigsberg was only a great critic.—

### 211.

I insist that we finally stop mistaking the workers in philosophy, and the scientific people generally, for philosophers, that this is the very point at which we must sternly give "to each his own," which means not too much to the former and not far too little to the latter. It may be necessary to the education of a genuine philosopher that he should have stood once on all the steps on which his servants, the scientific workers in philosophy, have now stopped —*must* have stopped; he himself must perhaps have been a critic and a skeptic and a dogmatist and a historian, not to mention poet, collector, traveller, riddle-reader, moralist, seer, "free thinker," and almost everything else, in order to run the entire circumference of human values and value-feelings, in order to be *able* to gaze with many eyes and many consciences from the heights to any distance, from the depths to any height, from the corners to any open spaces. But all these are only prerequisites for his task. The task itself is something else: it demands that he *create values*. Those philosophical workers in the noble tradition of Kant and Hegel have to determine and formalize some large reservoir of value-judgments, that is *former value-creations,*

which have come to the fore and for a certain
length of time are called "truth." They may lie in
the realm of logic or of politics (morality) or of
esthetics. The role of the researchers is to make
everything that has heretofore happened and been
evaluated into a visible, thinkable, comprehensible
and handy pattern; to abbreviate everything that is
long, to abbreviate time itself; to *overpower* the entire past. It is an enormous and wonderful task in
whose service any subtle pride and any tough will
may surely take satisfaction. *But the real philosophers are commanders and legislators.* They say,
"It *shall* be thus!" They determine the "whither"
and the "to what end" of mankind—having the
preliminary work of all the workers in philosophy,
the overpowerers of the past, at their disposal. But
they grope with creative hands toward the future—
everything that is and was becomes their means,
their instrument, their hammer. Their "knowing" is
*creating*. Their creating is legislative. Their will to
truth is—*will to power*. Are there such philosophers
today? Were there ever such philosophers? *Must*
there not be such philosophers? . . .

## 212.

It seems to me more and more that the philosopher, being *necessarily* a man of tomorrow and the
day after tomorrow, has at all times stood, and has
*had* to stand, in opposition to his today. His enemy
each time was the ideal of the day. All these extraordinary furtherers of mankind (who are called
philosophers but who rarely feel like lovers of wisdom, more like disagreeable fools and dangerous
question marks), have hitherto found their task,
their hard, unwanted, peremptory task—but ulti-

mately also the greatness of their task—in being the bad conscience of their time. By putting the vivi-sectionist's knife to the *virtues of their time,* they revealed their own secret: they knew a *new* magni-tude of man, a new un-worn path to his magnifica-tion. At all times they showed how much hypocrisy, indolence, letting oneself go and letting oneself fall, how many lies, were hidden under the most respected type of their current morality, how much virtue was out-lived. At all times they said, "We must go away, out there, where *you* today are least at home!" Faced with a world of "modern ideas" which would like to lock everyone into a corner and "specialty" of his own, a philosopher (if there could be philoso-phers today) would be forced to see the greatness of man, the very concept of "greatness," in all man's magnitude and multiplicity, in his "oneness in the many." He would determine human worth and rank by the amount and variety that an individual could carry within himself, by the *distance* his responsi-bility could span. The current taste and the current virtues weaken and adulterate the will today; noth-ing is as timely as weakness of will. Hence the phi-losopher must include strength of will, hardness, and ability to make far-reaching decisions in his ideal of human greatness. To this he has as much right as that with which the opposite teaching and the ideal of an abashed, renouncing, humble, self-less humanity was taught to an opposite era like the sixteenth century, for example, which suffered from a dammed up energy of the will and from the wildest torrents and flood waters of selfishness. At the time of Socrates, among men of fatigued instincts, among conservative Athenians who were letting themselves go—"for happiness," they said; for pleasure, their

conduct showed—who were still mouthing the old
magnificent phrases to which they had long forfeited
the right by their mode of life, among such men it
was perhaps *irony* that was necessary for greatness
of soul. What was needed was that malicious So-
cratic sureness of the old physician and plebeian
who cut into his own flesh as remorselessly as he
cut into the flesh and heart of "distinguished citi-
zens" with a look which said clearly enough, "Don't
pretend to me! At this point—we are equals!"
Today the opposite pertains. Today, when in Europe
the herd-animal alone is honored and alone doles
out the honors, when "equality of rights" could all
too easily turn into equality of wrong-doings—by
which I mean the joint war on everything rare,
strange, privileged; on superior men, superior souls,
superior duties, superior responsibilities, on creative
fullness of powers and the ability to rule—today
the concept of greatness must embrace the spirit
who is distinguished, who wants to be himself, who
can be different, who can stand alone, and who must
live by his own resources. A philosopher reveals
something of his own ideal when he legislates that
"The greatest shall be the one most capable of solitude, the most hidden, the most deviative, the man
beyond good and evil, the master of his virtues, the
one whose will can overflow. *Greatness* shall con-
sist in being as many-faceted as one is whole, as
wide as one is full." To ask the question once more:
is greatness today—possible?

### 213.

It is difficult to learn what constitutes a philosopher because it cannot be taught. One must "know"
it from one's own experience, or else have the

pride *not* to know it. But all the world today talks
about things which it *cannot* have experienced. And
this is most true, alas, of philosophers and all the
circumstances surrounding philosophy. Only the very
few know it, are permitted to know it, and all popular
opinion about it is wrong. That genuinely philosophical juxtaposition, for example, of a bold, exuberant spiritedness whose tempo is *presto,* and a
dialectical rigor and necessity which never makes
a misstep, is something unknown to the personal
experience of most thinkers and intellectuals. Hence,
if someone were to talk about it, they would only
find it incredible. They imagine every necessity as
a distress, as a painful having-to-obey and being-
compelled. Thinking seems to them something slow
and hesitant, almost a labor, and often enough
"worthy of the *sweat* of a noble man," but never
something light, divine, something closely related
to the dance and to playful high spirits. "Thinking"
and "taking something seriously," "taking it gravely,"
are to them the same thing: such is their personal
experience. Artists have a subtler sense of scent in
this respect. They know only too well that only
when they do nothing "willfully" and everything
"of necessity" does their feeling of freedom, subtlety, full powers, of creative placing, disposing,
and forming, reach its height. In short, that necessity and "freedom of the will" are one and the same
when they create. Ultimately there is an order of
rank in psychic conditions which approximates to the
order of rank in the problems to be solved. The most
superior problems mercilessly reject anyone who
dares approach them without being predestined, by
the superiority and power of his spirit, to solve them.
What good does it do if a nimble "cosmopolitan" in-

tellect, or a clumsy, decent mechanic or empiricist tries to penetrate the holy of holies with his plebeian ambitions, as happens so often today! Coarse feet simply cannot tread on this carpet: a basic primitive law sees to that. The gates remain closed to these importunate ones, no matter how hard they butt their heads against them, and even if they butt them bloody. One must be born to any superior world—to make it plainer, one must be *bred* for it. One has a right to philosophy (taking the word in its greatest sense) only by virtue of one's breeding. One's ancestors, one's "blood" decides this, too. Many generations must have worked on the origin of a philosopher; each one of his virtues must have been separately earned, cared for, passed on, made flesh and blood. This is true not only of the bold, light, delicate course and current of his thoughts, but above all of his willingness to undertake great responsibilities, of the grandeur with which his eyes rule and look downward, of his feeling that he is apart from the mass and their duties and virtues, of his courteous protection and defense of everything that is misunderstood and calumniated, whether it be God or the devil. It is true of his delight and practice in justice (in the high sense), of his skill in commanding, of the breadth of his will, of his slow eye which rarely admires, rarely looks up, rarely loves. . . .

# SEVENTH ARTICLE

## OUR VIRTUES

### 214.

Our virtues? It is probable that we have our virtues, too, although it is fair enough to predict that they will not be the good-hearted and four-square virtues for which we honor our grandfathers—and keep them at a little distance, too. We Europeans of the day after tomorrow, we first-lings of the twentieth century—with all our dangerous curiosity, our multiplicity and skill in disguising ourselves, our delicate and somewhat sweetened cruelty of spirit and senses—we, *if* we should have virtues, will only have those that have best learned to get along with our most secret and ardent inclinations, with our most fervent needs. Very well, let us look for such virtues in our labyrinths where, as everyone knows, so many things are lost and so many stay lost. Is there anything sweeter than *looking* for one's own virtues? Doesn't it almost amount to *believing* in one's own virtue? But this "belief in one's virtue"—isn't this basically what used to be called "good conscience," that honored, long-winded, conceptual queue[1] that our grandfathers used to attach to the back of their heads and often enough to the back of their minds! Thus it seems that however little we imagine ourselves to be old-fashioned and grandfatherly-respectable, we are nonetheless the worthy descendants of those grand-

---

[1] In Germany, old-fashioned and reactionary pedantry is called "queue," after the head-gear which was in vogue prior to the French Revolution. *Tr.*

fathers, we last Europeans with a good conscience. We too still wear their queue. Ah—if you knew how soon, how very soon, things will have changed!—

## 215.

As in the realm of the stars there are occasionally two suns which determine the orbit of one planet, as in certain cases, suns of different colors shine upon a single planet, flooding it sometimes with red, sometimes with green light and then again meeting upon its face and flooding it with many-colored light; so we modern men are determined by *different* moralities, thanks to the complicated mechanics of our "stellar sky." Our actions glow alternately with various colors; they are seldom unequivocal; and there are many cases in which we perform many-colored actions.

## 216.

To love one's enemies? This, I think, has been well learned. It happens today a thousand times, in little things and in big ones; sometimes, in fact, the superior and sublime thing happens: we learn to despise when we love, especially when we love best. But all this happens unconsciously, without noise, without pomp, with that modesty and secrecy of goodness that forbids our mouths to express the solemn word and the formula of virtue. Morality as an attitude today runs counter to our taste. This, too, is progress, just as it was our fathers' progress that religion as an attitude finally ran counter to their taste, including the hostility and Voltairean bitterness against religion (and whatever used to belong to the pantomime of freethinkers). It is the music in our conscience, the dance in our spirit, with which the Puritan litanies, the morality-preachments, and the "solid virtues" will not harmonize.

### 217.

Beware of all those who place a high value on being credited with moral tactfulness and subtlety of moral distinctions. They will never forgive us if they have once made a mistake in our presence (or, worse yet, about *us*). They unavoidably become our instinctive calumniators and detractors, even when they remain our "friends." Blessed are the forgetful, for they can forget even their stupidities.

### 218.

The French psychologists (and where can psychologists be found today except in France?) have still not had their fill of bitter and manifold pleasure in uncovering the *bêtise bourgeoise,*[2] almost as though. . . . In any event, they are revealing something about themselves. Flaubert, for example, the good citizen of Rouen, in the end saw, heard, and tasted nothing but this—it was his method of self-torture and refined cruelty. Now I should like to recommend (just for a change, for it gets boring) something else for people's delight: the unconscious astuteness with which all the good fat worthy mediocre minds behave toward superior minds and their tasks; the delicately interlaced jesuitical astuteness which is a thousand times more subtle than the intellect or taste of this middle class in even its best moments—far subtler also than the intellect

---

[2] Bourgeois stupidity.

of its victims. I offer this example in additional proof that "instinct" is the most intelligent of all the types of intelligence that have heretofore been discovered. In short, you psychologists, study the philosophy of the "rule" battling the "exception." There you have a spectacle worthy of the gods and of divine malice! Or, still more plainly, practice vivisection on "the good man," the "man of good will," . . . on *yourselves*.

### 219.

The making of moral judgments and condemnations is the favorite revenge of those of limited mind on those whose mind is less so; it is also a sort of compensation for having been ill-favored by nature; but ultimately it is an opportunity to *get* a mind and to *become* more subtle. For malice spiritualizes people. It does them good at the bottom of their hearts to know that there is a standard by which they and those who seem to them over-endowed with intellectual goods and privileges are measured alike. They battle for "equality before God" and for this they almost *need* to have faith in God. Among them are the strongest opponents of atheism. If someone were to say to them that "superior intellectual capacity cannot be compared with any sort of honesty and respectability of a merely moral man," it would set them to raving. I shall be very careful to say no such thing. Instead, I should like to flatter them with my proposition that superior intellectual capacity is itself only the final offshoot of moral qualities; that it is a synthesis of all those conditions reputed of a "merely moral" man, after they have one by one been earned through long discipline and practice, perhaps on the part of whole chains of generations; that superior intellectual ability consists of the spiritualization of justice and of the kindly severity which knows its task: to uphold the order of rank in the world, among things as well as among men.

### 220.

Now that the praise of "disinterestedness" has become so popular, we must bring up to consciousness, perhaps not without some risk, *what* the people are really interested in. What are the things which thoroughly and deeply concern the common man, including the educated, and even the intellectual and—if appearances do not deceive—the philosopher as well? We shall find the fact that the vast majority of things that interest and fascinate any superior nature, any subtler and more fastidious taste, seem totally "uninteresting" to the average man. If he nonetheless notices that certain people are devoted to such things, he calls it *"désintéressé,"* wondering how it is possible to act while "disinterested." There have been philosophers who knew how to give this popular astonishment a seductive and mystic-transcendental flavor (perhaps because they were not acquainted with a superior nature through personal experience), instead of giving out the naked and downright cheap truth that the "disinterested" action is a *very* interesting and interested action, provided that. . . . "How about love, then?" What? An act of love is supposed to be "unegoistic"? Why, you idiots. . . . "How about praising the one who sacrifices himself?" Whoever has really sacrificed anything, knows that he wanted and got something in return. Perhaps something on himself in return for something of himself. He knows that he yielded here in order to have more there, or perhaps in order to *be* more in general, or to feel like "more." But this is a field of questions and answers in which a fastidious intellect does not like to dwell. Truth has a terrible time to keep from yawning when it has to answer questions like these. Ultimately Truth is a woman: we must not violate her.

### 221.

It happens, said a moralistic pedant and small-shopkeeper, that I accord honor and distinction to a man who is not self-interested; but I do it not because he is not self-interested, but because he has a right, it seems to me, to be useful to others at his own expense. Enough: it is always a question of who *he* is and who *the other* is. Take, for example, someone who is destined and made for command: self-negation and diffidence would be not a virtue in him, but the wasting of a virtue, it seems to me. Every unselfish morality which takes itself as an absolute and seeks to apply itself to Everyman sins not only against taste, but does worse: it is an incentive to sins of omission; it is *one more* seduction under the guise of philanthropy; it seduces and harms precisely the superior, rare, privileged natures. One must force the moralities to subordinate themselves first of all to the principle of *rank;* one must make their conscience conscious of their arrogance—until they can finally understand and agree that it is *immoral* to say "What is right for one is right for the other."—To come back to my moralistic pedant and *bonhomme:* did he deserve being laughed at when he chided the moralities to be more moral? But one should never be too right if one would

have the laughers on *one's own* side; a little grain
of wrong is a necessary ingredient of good taste.

### 222.

Wherever compassion is being preached today
(and, heard aright, no other religion is being
preached anywhere), the psychologist should open
his ears. Through all the vanity, all the noise these
preachers make (like all preachers), he will hear
a hoarse, groaning, genuine sound of *self-contempt*.
It is part and parcel of that depression and uglification of Europe which has been going on for a century, *if, in fact, it is not the cause*. (Its first symptoms were documented in a thought-provoking letter
of Galiani to Madame d'Epinay.) The man of
"modern ideas," proud ape that he is, is uncontrol-
ably dissatisfied with himself: that much is certain.
He is suffering, but his vanity demands that he is
merely enduring "fellow-suffering,"—compassion.

### 223.

The hybrid European—a tolerably ugly plebeian,
all things considered—necessarily requires a cos-
tume. He needs history because it is the storage
closet in which the costumes are kept. He notices,
to be sure, that none really fits him—so he keeps
trying on more and more. Let us look at the nineteenth century with this in mind: our quick favorites
and equally quick discards among the styles; also
our moment of despair that "nothing suits us." It
seems no use pretending that we are romantic or
classical or Christian or Florentine or baroque or
"national," *in moribus et artibus:* we never look
well-dressed. But the "spirit," particularly the "historical spirit," can see an advantage in even its

despair: It can over and over again try on, wrap itself up in, take off again, and pack away another piece of primitive history or foreign manner. Above all, it can *study*. We are the first era that is truly learned so far as "costumes" are concerned—I mean moralities, articles of faith, esthetic tastes, and religions. We are better prepared than any time has ever been for the Great Carnival, the most spirited Mardi-Gras laughter, the most reckless fun, for the transcendental summit of the utmost idiocy, for a truly Aristophanean mockery of the universe. Perhaps we shall discover here the field for our kind of inventiveness, the field in which we too can be original! Perhaps we can be the parodists of world history, the punchinellos of God! If nothing else living today has a future—perhaps it will be our *laughter* that has one.

## 224.

*The historical sense* (or the ability to intuit quickly the order of rank among value-estimates according to which a nation or a society or a man has lived; the instinct for "divining" the interrelations of these value-estimates, for the relation of the authority of the values to the authority of the forces in operation)—the historical sense, which we Europeans claim as our special distinction, has come to us via the bewitching and insane half-barbarism into which Europe was plunged by the democratic upheaval of the castes and races. It is only the nineteenth century that knows this sense—as its sixth sense. The past of every form and mode of life, of cultures that formerly clashed—horizontally or vertically—is flowing into our "modern souls" thanks to that upheaval. Our instincts now can run back in all kinds of directions; we ourselves are a kind of chaos. But ultimately, as I have said, the mind seizes on its advantage. Through our half-barbarian bodies and desires we have all sorts of secret entry into places that were closed to any distinguished epoch, above all into the labyrinths of unfinished cultures, and of all the half-barbarisms that ever existed on earth. And since the greatest part of human culture heretofore has been half-barbaric, the "historical sense" really amounts to a sense and an instinct for everything, a taste and a tongue for everything—thus proving that it is an *undistinguished* sense. We can enjoy Homer once more, for example. Perhaps it is our happiest step forward that we can have a taste for Homer. It is a taste that the men of a distinguished culture (such as seventeenth century Frenchmen, for example, with their Saint-Evremond who accused Homer of *esprit vaste;*[3] even in their echo that was Voltaire) did not know how to acquire, a taste that they could hardly permit themselves to enjoy. The very definite "yes" and "no" of their taste buds, their easily called-forth nausea, their hesitant holding back from everything foreign, their disinclination for the dubious taste even of lively curiosity; in general, the ill will that every distinguished and self-sufficient culture has for admitting any new desire, any dissatisfaction with what is its own, any admiration of what is foreign—all this determines and disposes them unfavorably toward even the best things in the world if they are not their own, or at any rate could not be *made* their own. No sense makes less sense to such men than the historical sense, with its humble plebeian inquisitiveness. How true this is of the

[3] Spirit of boundlessness.

taste for Shakespeare—that astounding Spanish-Moorish-Saxon taste-synthesis at which an ancient Athenian in Aeschylus' circle would have either laughed or vexed himself sick! But we accept precisely this wild riot of color, this medley of utter delicacy, grossness, and artifice, with a secret sense of familiarity and love; we savor Shakespeare as though he were esthetic refinement personified, and especially saved up for us. The revolting vapors and closeness of the English rabble in which Shakespearean art and taste has its being disturbs us no more than, say, the Chiaja of Naples where we go along our way, willing and enchanted, with all our senses alive but quite oblivious of the cesspool odors wafting up from the lower town. We men of the historical sense have our virtues as such; this cannot be denied. We are unassuming, self-less, modest, brave, full of self-overcoming, full of devotion, very grateful, very patient, very amiable—though with all this we may not be very "tasteful." Let us finally admit to ourselves that what is hardest for us men of the historical sense to grasp, to feel, to taste, or to love, the thing that finds us basically prejudiced and almost hostile, is perfection, ultimate maturity, in a culture or an art. It is the essential quality of distinction in works and in men, their moment of calm sea and halcyon self-sufficiency, the goldenness and coldness exhibited by all things that have become perfect and complete. Perhaps the greatest virtue of our historical sense stands in necessary opposition to *good* taste, at least to the very best taste. Only poorly, hesitantly, only by compelling ourselves, can we capture in ourselves the image of the small, brief, and loftiest pieces of good fortune and of transfiguration in human life, as they send

out an occasional gleam here and there—those
moments and miracles when a great power voluntarily stopped before it ran out into measurelessness
and boundlessness, an overflow of subtle delight was
enjoyed in a sudden checking and turning to stone,
in the coming to a standstill on a ground that is still
trembling. *Measure* is foreign to us—let us admit
it. The stimulus that tickles us is the infinite, the
immeasurable. Like a rider on a forward-charging
horse, we drop our reins when infinity lies before
us, we modern men, we half-barbarians. We are
in the midst of *our* bliss only where we are most—
*in danger*.

### 225.

Whether it is hedonism, pessimism, utilitarianism,
or eudemonism—all these ways of thinking which
measure the value of things according to *pleasure*
and *pain,* i.e. according to subsidiary circumstances
and secondary considerations, are superficial ways
of thinking. They are naïvetés upon which anyone
who is conscious of *formative* powers and of an
artist's conscience will look with scorn and not
without some compassion. Compassion for *you!*
That is, to be sure, not the compassion you have in
mind. It is not compassion with "social distress,"
with "society" and its sick and maimed, with those
who are vice-laden and broken from their very
beginnings, as they lie strewn on the ground around
us; even less is it compassion with grumbling, oppressed, revolutionary slave strata who seek domination and call it "freedom." *Our* compassion is a
superior, more farsighted compassion. We see how
*mankind* is depreciating, how *you* are depreciating
mankind. There are moments in which we look with

indescribable anxiety at *your* compassion, when we defend ourselves against what you call compassion, when we find your earnestness more dangerous than any wantonness. You want, if possible (and there is no more insane "if possible") to *do away with suffering*. And we—it seems that *we* want it worse and more than it ever was! Well-being as you think of it is no aim; to us it seems more like an *end*—a finish! A condition which makes men ridiculous and contemptible, which creates the *desire* that man might perish. The discipline of suffering, of suffering in the *great* sense: don't you know that all the heightening of man's powers has been created by only this discipline? That tension of the soul in misfortune which trains it to strength, its shudders at the sight of great perdition, its inventiveness and courageousness in enduring, maintaining itself in, interpreting, and utilizing, misfortune—whatever was given to the soul by way of depth, mystery, mask, mind, guile, and greatness: was it not given through suffering, through the discipline of great suffering? In man there is united both *creature* and *creator;* in man there is material, fragment, excess, clay, filth, nonsense, and chaos. But in man there is also creator, image-maker, hammer-hardness, spectator-divinity, and day of rest: do you understand this antithesis? And do you understand that *your* compassion is spent on the "creature" in man, on that which must be formed, broken, forged, torn, burnt, brought to white heat, purified, on all that which must necessarily suffer and *ought* to suffer! And our compassion—don't you comprehend on whom our *opposite* compassion is spent, when it defends itself against your compassion, as though against the worst coddling and weakness? Compassion, in other words, against compassion!—But, as I said before, there are problems higher than any pleasure and pain problems, including that of the pain of compassion; any philosophy which seeks to culminate here is a naïveté.

### 226.

*We immoralists!* This world with which *we* are concerned, within which we fear and love, this almost invisible, inaudible world of subtle commands, subtle obedience, this world of "almost" in every sense, this touchy, deceptive, pointed, and delicate world: how well it is defended against gross spectators and familiar curiosity! We are spun into a strict network and hairshirt of duties; we *cannot* get out. In this we are men of "duty," even we. At times, true enough, we dance in our "chains" and among our "swords." More often, no less true, we grit our teeth in impatience at the secret hardness of our lot. But do what we will—the idiots and their "eye-witness" evidence speak against us: these are men *without duties,* they say. We always have the idiots and the evidence of their eyes against us.

### 227.

Candor: granted that this is the virtue from which we free thinkers cannot escape. Well, let us work on this virtue in all malice and all love. Let us not weary of "perfecting" *our* virtue, the only one left to us. Let its glow some day rest on this aging culture and its dull gloomy earnestness, like a golden, blue, mocking after-glow. But if our candor, nonetheless, grows tired one day, and sighs and stretches its limbs and finds us too hard and would like to have something better, easier, more tender, something like a pleasant vice, then let us remain *hard,* we last Stoics! Let us send to our candor's aid whatever devilment we possess: our nausea at grossness and lack of definition, our *nitimur in vetitum,*[4] our adventurous courage, our quick-witted and fastidious inquisitiveness, our subtlest, most disguised, most spiritual will to power and world-overcoming, that roams and flutters desirously about all the fields of the future. Let us come to the aid of our "god" with all our "devils"! Most probably we shall be misunderstood and not recognized for what we are, but what does it matter! They will say that "their candor is their very devilishness, and nothing but that"—what does it matter! And even if they were right—were not all gods once devils, only re-christened and become holy? And in the end, what do we know about ourselves? Or about what the spirit who guides us wants to be *called* (for it is a question of naming)! Or how many spirits we contain? Our candor—we free thinkers—let us see to it that it doesn't turn into our vanity, our ornament and ostentation, our limitation, our stupidity! Every virtue inclines toward stupidity; every stupidity toward virtue. "Stupid to the point of holiness," they say in Russia. Let us see to it that we don't turn into saints and bores from sheer candor! Isn't life a hundred times too short to be bored with it? One would really have to believe in the life everlasting in order to. . . .

### 228.

I trust I shall be forgiven for the discovery that all moral philosophy hitherto was boring and belonged among the soporifics, that virtue has been

---

[4] Striving for the forbidden.

more impaired, in my eyes, by its boring proponents
than by anything else—which is not to say that I
fail to recognize the general utility of such proponents. Much depends on it, that as few people
as possible should reflect on morality. Hence *very*
much depends on it that morality should not by any
chance become interesting! But we need not worry.
Things today stand where they have always stood:
I see no one in Europe who has (or could give to
anyone else) the slightest conception that reflecting
about morality might proceed dangerously, insidi-
ously, seductively—that *doom* might lie in it! Look
for example at the indefatigable, inescapable British
Utilitarians; how ponderously and respectably they
walk back and forth (a Homeric metaphor says it
more plainly) in the footsteps of Bentham, just as
Bentham followed in the footsteps of the respectable
Helvetius (no—he was not a dangerous man, this
Helvetius: *ce sénateur Pococurante,* Galiani called
him). Not a new thought, not a subtler turn or fold
of an old thought, not even a real history of former
thoughts: an *impossible* literature, on the whole,
unless one knows how to pickle it for oneself in a
certain amount of malice. For into these moralists
too (between whose lines one must read if one must
read them at all) has crept that old British vice
which is called *cant* and which is *moral Tartuffery,*
only this time hidden under the new form of scientific method. Furthermore, there is no lack of the
secret struggle with their consciences, from which a
race of former Puritans (as is fair and proper) will
always suffer when they show a scientific concern
for morality. (Is a moralist not the counterpart of
a Puritan? A man, that is, who takes morality
as something questionable, questionmark-worthy, in

short, problematic? Isn't moralizing—immoral?) In the end they all want to prove that British morality is right, insofar as humanity or the "general welfare" or the "happiness of the greatest number"—nay, the happiness of *England* is best served by it. With all their powers they like to prove to themselves that the striving for *British* happiness (by this I mean comfort, fashion, and, at the highest level, a seat in Parliament) is at the same time the proper path to virtue. That, in fact, whatever virtue there has been in the world, consisted of such striving. None of all these herd animals, clumsy and conscience-pricked as they are, who espouse the cause of egoism as the cause of the general welfare, wants to have an insight into or even catch a whiff of the fact that the general welfare is not an ideal, not an aim, not a comprehensible concept even, but only an emetic. That which is fair to one *cannot* by any means be fair to another. The demand of one morality for all means an encroachment upon precisely a superior type of man. There is, in short, an order of rank between men and hence also between moralities. They are a modest and thoroughly mediocre type, these Utilitarian Britons, and, as I said before, insofar as they are boring, one cannot think too highly of their utility. One should in fact *encourage* them, as I try to do in the following rhymes:

Hail you worthy molehill climbers,[5]
Ever "take-your-own-sweet-timers,"
Growing stiff in head and knee.

[5] The "molehill climbers" are "pushcart peddlers" in Nietzsche. They were here sacrificed for the sake of the casual and reckless rhyming of which Nietzsche was so fond. *Translator*

Soul of washrag, face of poker,
Overwhelming-mediocre,
*Sans génie et sans esprit!*

### 229.

In those late epochs which have a right to be proud of their humane sentiments, there remains so much fear, so much *superstitious* fear of the "wild cruel beast" whose conquest constitutes the pride of their humane sentiments, that even palpable truths remain unexpressed for centuries, as though by general agreement, because they look as though they might revive that wild, finally slaughtered, beast. So I am risking something perhaps, if I let one such truth out of my hands. But let others capture it again and give it enough milk of human kindness to drink until it lies quietly and forgotten in its old corner once more.—We should relearn our lesson on cruelty and open our eyes. We should finally learn impatience with the immodest and fat errors that are virtuously and impudently making their way among us, such as the error in regard to tragedy for example, which has been force-fed by new and old philosophers alike. Practically everything that we call "superior culture" rests on the intellectualization and deepening of *cruelty:* this is my proposition. This is the wild beast that was not slaughtered at all; it lives; it flourishes; it has only been—deified. What constitutes the painful delight of tragedy is cruelty; what is pleasurable in so-called tragic pity, and basically in everything sublime right up to the highest and subtlest thrills of metaphysics, gets its sweetness from nothing other than the added ingredient of cruelty. What the Roman enjoys in

the Arena, the Christian in the ecstasies of the cross,
the Spaniard in the sight of the stake and the bull-
fight, the modern Japanese who is drawn to tragedy,
the worker in the suburbs of Paris who feels nostalgia for bloody revolutions, the female Wagnerian
with will suspended who lets *Tristan und Isolde*
"come over" her—what they all enjoy and seek to
incorporate into themselves with a secret passionate
ardor is the magic brew of the great Circe *Cruelty*.
Naturally we must get rid of the old ridiculous
psychology which knew no better than to teach that
cruelty only arises at the sight of *someone else's* suffering. There is a rich, an over-rich pleasure in one's
own suffering, in making oneself suffer. Wherever
man is persuaded to self-negation in the religious
sense, or to self-mutilation as among the Phoenicians
and ascetics, or to any form of de-sensualization, de-
carnalization, contrition, to Puritanical repentance-
paroxysms, to vivisection of the conscience, to
Pascal-like *sacrifizio dell' intelletto*—there he is
secretly lured and propelled by his cruelty, by the
dangerous thrills of cruelty *inflicted on himself*.
Ultimately, we must consider that even the man of
insight—insofar as insight is paid for by the mind's
opposition to its own inclinations, and often by its
opposition to one's heart's desires, by its forcing one
to say "no" where one would like to say "yes," to
love, to adore—that such a man, too, operates as
an artist and a transfigurer of cruelty. Any depth,
any thoroughness is already a violation, a desire to
hurt the basic will of man's mind whose trend is
constantly toward illusion, toward the surface. In
any desire of the mind to penetrate deeply and with
understanding there is already a drop of cruelty.

## 230.

Perhaps what I have just said about the "basic will of the mind" will not be readily understood, so that I may be permitted an elucidation.—The command-giving something which is called "mind" by the people wants to be master in itself and all around itself and to feel that it is master. It has the will to make simplicity out of multiplicity; it is a will that ties things up, tames them—a domineering and really dominant will. Its needs and capabilities are the same as those which the physiologists assign to everything that lives and grows and reproduces. The power of mind to absorb foreign elements reveals itself in its strong tendency to make the new like the old, to simplify the manifold, to overlook or reject the totally contradictory; mind also arbitrarily underlines, emphasizes, falsifies—in order to suit its own purposes—certain features and characteristics of things foreign to itself, i. e. every bit of "outside world" that comes into its ken. Its purpose is the incorporation of new "experiences," the adding of new material to old, its *growth* in other words, or more strictly defined, the *feeling* of its growth, the feeling of its increased power. A servant of this same will is an apparently opposite drive of the mind: a suddenly erupting decision to be ignorant, to be arbitrarily shut off, a closing of windows, an inward "no" to this or that, a refusal to be approached, a sort of defense against much that might be known, a satisfaction at being in the dark, at being enclosed within a limiting horizon, a "yes" and a benediction upon ignorance—all according to the present needs of its appropriating power, its "digestive power, metaphorically speaking. Really, the mind is more like a stomach than anything else. Furthermore we must add the occasional will of the mind to be deceived, perhaps with a reckless intuition that things are *not* this way or that, that one is simply taking them for this or that, a delight in insecurity and ambiguity, a gay self-satisfaction in the arbitrary narrowness and secrecy of a given corner, in the all-too-near, the foreground, the magnified, the minimized, the distorted, the beautified— a self-satisfaction in the arbitrary nature of all such expressions of power. And finally there is that precarious willingness of the mind to deceive other minds and to disguise itself; that constant pressure and impulsion of a creative, image-making, changeable power: in this, the mind enjoys its many masks, its cunning; also the feeling of its own security, for it is best defended and concealed by its Proteusskills. Counter to *this* will to illusion, to simplification, to the mask, to the cloak, in short this will to surfaces (for every surface is a cloak) operates that sublime impulse of the man of insight, that spirit which takes and *wants* to take things deeply, complicatedly, and thoroughly. This is the cruelty characteristic of the intellectual conscience and taste. Every courageous thinker will acknowledge it in himself, provided that he has trained and sharpened his eyes for it long enough, as is proper, and is accustomed to rigorous discipline and to rigorous words as well. He will say "There is something cruel about the tendency of my mind," regardless of the virtuous and amiable people who will try to dissuade him! Indeed, it would sound prettier if they talked about us or whispered after us or admired us in terms of "excessive candor," let us say, instead of cruelty. We free, *very* free thinkers—perhaps that will be our posthumous reputation! Meanwhile—and a long while it will be—we should be the least inclined to ornament ourselves with such moralistic word-spangles and bangles. Our entire work ruins us for that sort of taste and its cheerful lushness. They are beautiful, glittering, jingling, festive words: candor, love for truth, love for wisdom, self-sacrifice for insight, heroism of the truthful! Something about them swells one's pride. But we anchorites and marmots, we have convinced ourselves long ago, in all the secrecy of our anchorite's conscience, that this worthy word-pomp too belongs to the old lying bangles, to all the deceptive junk and gold dust of unconscious human vanity; that even beneath such flattering colors and cosmetics the frightful basic text *homo natura,* must be recognized for what it is. For to retranslate man back into nature, to master the many vain enthusiastic glosses which have been scribbled and painted over the everlasting text, *homo natura,* so that man might henceforth stand before man as he stands today before that *other* nature, hardened under the discipline of science, with unafraid Oedipus eyes and stopped up Ulysses ears, deaf to the lures of the old metaphysical bird catchers who have been fluting in at him all too long that "you are more! You are superior! You are of another origin!"—this may be a strange, mad task, but who could deny that it is a *task!* Why did we choose it, this mad task? Or, to ask it with different words, "Why insight, anyway?" Everyone will ask us this. And we, pressed for an answer, having asked the same question of ourselves hundreds of times, we have found and shall find no better answer. . . .

## 231.

Learning transforms us. It does what all nutrition does, namely much more than merely "maintain," as the physiologists know. But fundamentally, "way down below" in us, there is something unteachable, a bedrock of intellectual destiny, of predestined decision, of answers to predestined, selected questions. In the presence of every cardinal problem there speaks an unchangeable "This is myself." On the problem man-woman, for example, a thinker cannot relearn anything but only learn to the end—only discover fully what is "in him." At certain times we find certain solutions to problems which create a strong faith in *us* in particular; one will perhaps call them one's convictions. Later, one sees in them only the footprints leading to self-understanding, the signposts pointing to the problem which *we are,* more correctly, to the great stupidity which we are, to our intellectual destiny, to the *unteachable* "way down below."—Considering this excessive courtesy which I have just committed against myself, I shall perhaps be permitted to speak aloud several truths about woman "as such." I assume that everyone now understands how much these truths are only—*my* truths.—

## 232.

Women want to become independent. To this end they are beginning to enlighten men about "women as such." This is one of the worst aspects of progress in the general uglification of Europe. For what all will not the clumsy attempts of feminine science and self-exposure bring to light! Women have so much cause for modesty; there is so much in women that is pedantic, superficial, school-marmish, petty-presumptuous, petty-unbridled, and petty-overbearing (just study their relations with children!), all of which was best repressed and limited by their *fear* of men. Woe to all of us when the "eternal bore" in women—they are full of it—dares come out! When women thoroughly and principally unlearn their cleverness and their art which consists of grace, playfulness, the ability to chase away cares, to make things easy and take things easy; when they forget their subtle adaptability to pleasant needs. Today we are hearing feminine voices which—by Saint Aristophanes—give us the horrors. With medical outspokenness they are threatening to tell what women *want*, first and last, from men. Is it not in the worst of taste when women thus go about becoming scientific? Hitherto, fortunately, enlightenment was a man's affair, a man's talent, and men remained "among themselves" with it. But in the end, when we read what women write about "woman," we are justified in a good measure of distrust that women really want—really *can* want—enlightenment about themselves. When a woman isn't merely seeking a new ornament for herself (I imagine that self-ornamentation goes with the eternal-feminine), well, perhaps she wants people to be afraid of her, perhaps she wants to dominate. But she surely does *not* want truth: what do women care for truth! Nothing, from the very beginning of things, is more foreign, more repulsive, more inimical to women than truth. Her great art is the lie; her highest concern is for appearances, for beauty (i.e. deception). Why don't we men admit it: we honor and love precisely that art, that instinct, in women; we, who have our diffi-

culties and who like the relief of associating with
beings beneath whose hands and looks and tender
follies our own earnestness, our gravity and profundity, almost seem like follies themselves. Let me
put this final question: Has a woman ever admitted
profundity in another woman's mind or justice
in another woman's heart? And isn't it true that,
by and large, "woman" was most despised by other
women, and not at all by us?—We men wish that
women would stop compromising themselves with
their enlightenment. It was masculine care and
masculine consideration for women that made the
church decree: *mulier taceat in ecclesia!* [6] It was
to the benefit of women when Napoleon made the
all too vocal Madame de Staël understand that
*Mulier taceat in politics.* [7] And I think that it would
be a genuine friend of women who would call out
to them today: *mulier taceat de muliere!* [8]

### 233.

It reveals corruption of the instincts (in addition
to poor taste) when a woman points to Madame
Roland or Madame de Staël or Monsieur George
Sand as proving something in *favor* of "woman as
such." Among men these three are the three *comic*
women as such, and nothing more! They are the
best involuntary arguments *against* emancipation
and feminine autonomy.

### 234.

Stupidity in the kitchen: woman as cook: the
gruesome thoughtlessness with which the nutrition

---

[6] Women should be silent in church.
[7] Women should be silent on the subject of politics.
[8] Women should be silent on the subject of women.

of the family and of the head of the house is carried
on! Women do not understand what food *means,*
and yet they want to do the cooking! If woman
were a thinking creature, she would have had to
come upon the most important physiological facts,
cook as she was for millenniums. She would have
appropriated the whole of medicine as her proper
domain. Because of bad cooking, because of the
perfect lack of rationality in the kitchen, human
development has been stunted for the longest time,
influenced in the worst conceivable way. And today
things are not much better. (A speech for "finish-
ing school" graduates.)

### 235.

There are turns and lucky finds of the spirit;
there are sentences, small handfuls of words, in
which a complete culture, a whole society, is suddenly crystallized. Among these is the casual remark of Madame de Lambert to her son: *"Mon ami,
ne vous permettez jamais que de folies, qui vous
feront grand plaisir."* [9] The most motherly and wise
remark, incidentally, that was ever addressed to
a son.

### 236.

What Dante and Goethe believed of women,
Dante with his *"ella guardava suso, ed io in lei,"* [10]
Goethe, translating it with *"Das Ewig-Weibliche
zieht uns hinan"* [11] I have no doubt that any superior
woman will defend herself against such belief. For

[9] My dear, never permit yourself any follies except
those that give you great pleasure.
[10] She looked upwards, and he to her.
[11] The eternal-feminine draws us upward.

it is *exactly* what she believes of the eternal-masculine. . . .

## 237.

### SEVEN LITTLE WOMAN-APHORISMS

How our greatest boredom flees,
When man comes crawling on his knees.

\* \* \*

Age, alas, and knowledge grey
Make even weak virtue go a long way.

\* \* \*

A good black dress, a tongue at rest,
Makes any woman look—well dressed.

\* \* \*

To whom I'm grateful when I'm gay?
To God—and my *couturier*.

\* \* \*

Young: a rosy cozy cell,
Old: a dragon raising hell.

\* \* \*

Handsome leg, well-bred name,
Male besides: I'll stake my claim.

\* \* \*

Speech that's brief, sense that's nice,
Has she-asses skating on thin ice.

Women have hitherto been treated by men as
though they were birds, as though they had lost their
way coming from higher regions, as though they
were something more delicate, more vulnerable,
more wild, strange, sweet and soulful—but something which must be caged to keep it from flying
off again.

## 238.

To be wrong on the fundamental problem man-woman, to deny the abysmal antagonism, the necessity of a forever hostile tension, to dream of equal rights, equal education, equal claims and obligations—is a *typical* sign of short-sightedness. A thinker who proves short-sighted in this dangerous spot, shallow in instinct, should be looked upon with suspicions, and more; he should be considered revealed, uncovered! He will probably prove too "short" for all the basic questions of life, including the life of the future, and unable to penetrate *any* depth! A man who has depth, on the other hand, depth of mind as well as of desires, and also that depth of good will which is capable of rigor and hardness (and is easily mistaken for them)—such a man can only think *orientally* about women. He *must* comprehend women as a possession, a property that can be closed off, as something predestined for service and thereby fulfilling its nature. He must place himself on the side of Asia's enormous rationality, Asia's superior instincts, just as the Greeks did, the best heirs and disciples of Asia. As is well known, the Greeks became gradually and increasingly strict, i.e. oriental, with women, as their culture increased in extent and strength, between the times of Homer and of Pericles. *How* necessary this was, *how* logical, *how* humanly desirable, even: let each man reflect upon by himself!

### 239.

At no other epoch has the weaker sex been treated with such respect by men as in ours; it is part of our democratic inclination and fundamental taste, exactly like our lack of respect for the aged. No wonder that such respect is immediately misused.

One wants more, one learns to make demands, one feels the very degree of respect as practically an insult; one would prefer to compete for rights, in fact one prefers open warfare: enough, women are losing all their shame. Let us add immediately that they are also losing their taste. They unlearn to *fear* man; but a woman who has "unlearned fear" is yielding her most feminine instincts. It is fair and comprehensive enough that woman dares to emerge when that which inspires fear—let us say the *man* in man—is no longer desired by society and hence no longer trained into being. What is harder to comprehend is that in this process woman herself degenerates. This is what is happening today; let us not deceive ourselves! Wherever the industrial spirit has triumphed over the military and aristocratic spirit, women are now striving for the economic and legal independence of an office boy. "Woman as office boy" is imprinted over the portal of modern society as it is emerging. But while women are seizing these new rights, while they are seeking to become "master" and writing "woman's progress" on their flags and rags, the opposite is taking place with frightful obviousness: *Woman is retrogressing.* In Europe since the French Revolution, the influence of women has *waned* to the degree to which their rights and claims have increased. And the "emancipation of women", insofar as it is demanded and furthered by women themselves (not merely by shallow male minds) thus shows itself as a peculiar symptom of the increased weakening and dulling of the most feminine instincts. There is *stupidity* in this movement, an almost masculine stupidity, for which a well-made woman (who is always a clever woman) ought to be deeply ashamed. To lose one's scent for the ground on which one could most surely win; to neglect one's practice with one's own proper weapons; to let oneself go in the presence of a man—perhaps as far as "the book"; whereas formerly one disciplined oneself into a subtle, wily humility; to work with virtuous audacity against man's belief in a basically different ideal that is *veiled* in women, his belief in something forever and necessarily feminine; to dissuade man, emphatically and vocally, that woman should be maintained, cared for, protected, and treated with consideration, like a more delicate, wondrously wild and often pleasant domestic pet; to collect, clumsily and indignantly, all the aspects of slavery and bondage that have adhered and still adhere to woman's position in society (as though slavery were a counterargument instead of a necessary condition for any superior culture, for any heightening of culture)— what does all this signify, if not a disintegration of the feminine instincts, a masculinization! There are enough idiotic woman-friends and woman-corrupters, to be sure, among the learned he-asses, who advise women to de-feminize themselves and to imitate all the stupidities from which "man" in Europe, all European "masculinity" suffers. They would no doubt like to pull women down to the level of the "general culture"; all the way down to newspaper reading and politicalizing. Now and again they even want to make a freethinker and "literary man" out of a woman, as though a woman without piety were not completely repulsive or ridiculous to a profound and godless man. Almost everywhere they ruin her nerves with the sickliest and most dangerous music (our latest German music) and make her daily more hysterical and less and less capable of her first and last professional activity, the bearing of healthy children. They want to make her more "cultivated" than ever (they call it strengthening the weaker sex through culture), as though history didn't teach us as insistently as possible that man's "cultivatedness" and man's weakness, i.e. the weakening, splintering, and sickliness of the *willpower*, have always kept in step. As though they didn't know that the most powerful and influential women in the world (Napoleon's mother was the last of them) owe their power and their superiority over man precisely to their willpower, not to any schoolmasters! What makes us respect and sometimes even fear a woman is her *nature* which is more "natural" than a man's; her genuine jungle-like wily flexibility, her tiger's claw beneath the glove, her naive egoism, her uneducability and inward wildness, the uncomprehensible wide sweep of her desires and virtues. . . . And what makes us compassionate toward this dangerous and beautiful great cat called Woman, even if we fear her, is that she is more capable of suffering, more vulnerable, more in need of love and doomed to disappointments than any other animal. Fear and compassion: these are the feelings that man has always had for woman, always one foot already in a tragedy that rends him as it enraptures. Really? And all this should now be at an end? And they are working against the *enchantress* in woman? The bore in woman is slowly emerging? Oh Europe, Europe! We know the beast with horns that was always so attractive to you, that was always your danger! [12] Your old fable is in danger of becoming "history."

[12] Nietzsche alludes to the Greek fable of Europa and the Bull. *Tr.*

Once again an enormous stupidity may become your master and carry you off! And this time there is no god hidden under it—only an "idea," a "modern idea!"—

# EIGHTH ARTICLE

## PEOPLES AND FATHERLANDS

### 240.

I heard, once again for the first time, Richard Wagner's overture to *Die Meistersinger,* a piece of magnificent, over-loaded, heavy and late art. It prides itself on presupposing two centuries of music as still living, in order to be understood; it honors the Germans that such a pride was not miscalculated! What saps, what energies, what seasons and climates, are here mingled! It impresses us as being now old-fashioned, now foreign; now acrid, now over-youthful; it is as arbitrary as it is pompous-traditional; it is frequently roguish, still more often rude and coarse; it has fire and courage and at the same time the flabby dun-colored skin of fruits that ripen too late. It flows broad and full; then suddenly a moment of inexplicable hesitation, a gap as it were opens between cause and effect; a pressure causing us to dream, almost a nightmare; but right away it broadens and widens anew, the old stream of gratification —the most manifold gratification, of old and new happiness, including *very much* the joy of the artist in himself, which he refuses to conceal, his astonished happy realization of his mastery of the means he employs, the new, newly acquired, as yet untested artifices which he seems to reveal to us. All in all there is no beauty, no South, nothing of the Southern delicate brightness of sky, nothing of grace, no dance, hardly a will to logic; in fact a certain grossness especially emphasized, as though the artist wished to say that it is part of his intention; a cumbersome drapery, something arbitrary, barbaric and solemn, a flittering of learned and venerable preciosities and pointedness; something German in the worst and best sense of the word, something manifold, disproportionate, and inexhaustible, German style, a certain German potency and excess of soul which is not afraid to hide beneath the refinements of decadence, in fact feels itself perhaps most at ease there; a real, genuine token of the German soul which is simultaneously young and aged, over-ripe and still over-rich in futurity. It is the kind of music that best expresses what I think of Germans: they are of the day before yesterday and the day after tomorrow—*as yet they have no today*.

### 241.

We "good Europeans": we too have our hours when we allow ourselves some cordial patriotic drivel, a plop and a relapse into old loves and old straits. (I have just given an example of it in the last section.) We have our hours of national throbbings, of patriotic wheezings, and all sorts of other old-fashioned floods of sentiment. More ponderous minds than ours may take much longer periods to get through with what takes us hours and is over in hours. Some may take half a year, others half a lifetime, depending on the speed and strength with which their digestion, their metabolism works. I could imagine dull sluggish faces which would need, even in our swift Europe, whole half centuries before they could overcome such atavistic attacks of patriotic and glued-to-the-native-soil drivel, and return to reason, i.e. to "good Europeanism." And as I was digressing on this possibility, it happened that I became an ear-witness to a conversation between two old "patriots." They were both obviously hard of hearing and therefore were shouting all the louder. "*That man* knows and cares as much about philosophy as a peasant or a fraternity boy," said the one, "he is still innocent. But what does it matter today? It is the time for the masses; they crawl on their belly before anything that is massive. And the same is true of politics. A statesman who builds them a new Tower of Babel, some new monstrosity of a nation and of power, is called 'great.' What do we matter, we more cautious and reserved ones, who are not yet ready to part with our belief that it is the great thought alone which imparts greatness to a deed or a cause. Supposing that a statesman put his people in the position where they had to play 'high politics,' but that they were a people not fitted by nature and ill-prepared to play this game. It would be necessary to sacrifice many old secure virtues for love of a new dubious mediocrity. Now supposing that a statesman condemned his people to 'politicking' as such, whereas that people had better things to do, and at the bottom of their soul were cautiously disgusted with the restiveness, the emptiness, the noisy wrangling of the politicking nations; supposing such a statesman goaded and pricked the half-asleep passions and greeds of his people, convinced them that their previous bashfulness and pleasure in being a spectator was a blot on their pride, made them feel guilty of their love for foreign places, their secret passion for infinities, devaluated their warmest inclinations for them, turned their consciences inside out, narrowed down their minds, 'nationalized' their taste—what? Such a statesman, for whom his people would have to do penance far into the future (if any future at all were left to them after him), such a

*CONDEMNATION OF HITLER*

statesman you would call 'great'?"—"Undoubtedly,"
answered the second old patriot violently. "If he were
not great, he couldn't have *done* it. Maybe you'll say
it was insane to *want* to do such a thing. But perhaps
all great things look insane at the beginning!"—
"Misuse of words," shrieked the other, "strong—
strong—strong—and insane. But *not* great!"—The
old men had obviously become heated as they were
thus shouting their "truths" in one another's face.
But I, happy in my Beyond, considered how quickly
a strong man will be mastered by a stronger man.
And how there is a compensation for the increasing
spiritual shallowness of a people: another people
will become deeper.

### 242.

Call it "civilization" or "humanization" or "progress"—this present-day distinction which is being
sought for Europeans; or call it simply, without praise
or blame, by its political formula: the democratic
movement in Europe. Behind all the moral and political foregrounds which such formulas designate, there
is going on an immense *physiological* process whose
current is running strong. The process of the mutual
assimilation of Europeans, their growing separation
from the conditions which give rise to climatically
determined and caste-bound races, their increasing
independence of any *definite* milieu that would seek
to inscribe itself on their bodies and souls with centuries of unvarying demands. In other words, the
gradual appearance of an essentially supra-national
and nomadic type of human being who, physiologically speaking, has a maximum of adaptability as his
typical excellence. This process of the "European in
progress" might be slowed up by some great relapses,

*Handwritten marginal notes:*

SUPERMEN ARE CONSTANTLY COMING - NO SUCH THING AS PROGRESS - JUST TEMPORARY CHANGE - WHY BOTHER HAVING IDOLS?

NOT CASTE BUT HERD - TO ADAPTABILITY

SOUGHT ALTROUGH TO ADAPTABILITY

LACK OF ARISTOCRACY.

GETTING AWAY FROM NARROWNESS OF
NATION BUT XTENDING NARROWNESS WORLD WIDE

but it would more than gain in vehemence and depth what it might lose in time. The still raging storm and stress of "national feelings" is one of these forces, likewise the presently emerging anarchism. The whole process will probably end with results least expected by its naive furtherers and admirers, the apostles of "modern ideas." The same new conditions which will, on the average, bring about an equalization and mediocritization of man, a useful, hardworking, adaptable herd-animal of many uses, are also disposed in the highest degree to the creation of exceptional men of most dangerous and fascinating quality. For while the adaptability which is constantly tested in changing conditions and which begins its work anew with each generation, almost with each decade, offers no possibility for a *powerful type;* while the total impression that these future Europeans will make will probably be one of manifold, gossipy, willpower-poor and extremely employable workers who *need* a boss, a master who gives them commands, as they need their daily bread; while, in other words, the democratization of Europe will amount to the creation of a type prepared in the subtlest sense for *slavery*—the individual, meanwhile, the exceptional case, the *strong* man, will turn out to be stronger and richer than he has probably ever been, thanks to the lack of prejudice in his schooling, thanks to the enormous varied practice he can get in skills and disguises. I meant to say that the democratization of Europe is at the same time an involuntary arrangement for the training of tyrants—taking the word in every sense, including its most intellectual.

## 243.

I am pleased to hear that our sun is moving

*[margin annotations, handwritten:]* A MASTER WILL RISE EASILY FROM IT

DEMOCRACY = STRONG SLAVE CLASS ↓ ADAPTABILITY

↗ ALLOW FOR HIGHER NA SHEPHERD TO COME

rapidly toward the constellation of *Hercules;* I hope
that man on this earth will imitate the sun in this.
And we foremost, we good Europeans!—

*[handwritten: SUPER-STRENGTH]*

*[handwritten: THOSE IN THE KNOW - WHO]*

244. *[handwritten: RESPECT ~~REGION~~ COUNT]*

There was a time when people were accustomed
to calling the Germans "deep" by way of distinction.
Now, when the most successful type of modern German is greedy for quite different honors and misses
"smartness" in anything deep, one is almost timely
and patriotic with one's doubt whether one was not
formerly deceived by such praise, whether German
depth is not at bottom some quite different and quite
bad thing; whether one shouldn't thank God that one
stands a chance of successfully getting rid of it. Let
us try, then, to relearn some things about German
profundity. All we need is a little vivisection of the
German psyche.—The German psyche is above all
multiple, of various sources, more put together and
superimposed than actually built. This is due to its
origin. A German who would be brash enough to
assert that "Two souls, alas, dwell in my breast,"
would fall woefully short of the truth by a number
of souls. As a people of a monstrous mixture and
conglomeration of races, perhaps even with a pre-
ponderance of a pre-Aryan element, as a people "of
the middle" in every sense, the Germans are less
palpable, more extensive, more contradictory, more
unknown, incalculable, surprising, even horrifying,
than other peoples are to themselves. They escape
*definition* and in this alone they are the despair of
the French. Characteristic of the German is that his
question "What is German?" never dies out. Kotzebue
surely knew his Germans well enough: "We have

been recognized," they cried joyfully—but Sand too thought they could be known. Jean Paul knew what he was doing when he furiously declared himself to be against Fichte's lying but patriotic flatteries and exaggerations. But it is probable that Goethe thought quite differently about the Germans, even though he agreed with Jean Paul so far as Fichte was concerned. What did Goethe think about the Germans, anyway? But he never spoke plainly about a great many things close to him; all his life he knew how to maintain a subtle silence—probably for good reasons. Certain it is that it wasn't the "Wars of Liberation" that made him look up happily, nor the French Revolution. The event for which he *reconsidered* his *Faust,* the whole problem of man, in fact, was the appearance of Napoleon. There are words of Goethe's in which he denies, as though from a foreigner's point of view, what the Germans point to with pride. He once defined the famous German soul (*Germüt*) as "indulgence with their own and others' weaknesses." Was he wrong? It characterizes the Germans that one is seldom completely wrong about them. The German psyche contains corridors within corridors; there are caves and hiding places and dungeons in it; its disorder has something of the enchantment of a mystery; the German knows how to creep on invisible paths to chaos. And as everything loves its symbol, so the German loves the clouds, everything that is unclear, evolving, twilit, damp, and overcast. Everything uncertain, unformed, self-displacing, and growing, he feels as "deep." The German himself *is* not; he *becomes;* he "evolves." "Evolution" is the truly German find in the great realm of philosophic formulas, a ruling concept which, in alliance with German beer and German music, is working on the Germanization of Europe. Foreigners stand astonished and fascinated before the riddles that the contradictory nature at the bottom of the German psyche gives them to read (a nature which Hegel systematized and Wagner translated even into music). "Good-natured and mean"—such a juxtaposition which would be nonsensical in reference to any other nation, is unfortunately too often justified in Germany. Just live among Swabians for a while! The ponderousness of the German intellectual, his social bad taste, can accompany horrifyingly easily an inward acrobatic and nimble boldness which all gods have already learned to fear. If one wants the German psyche demonstrated before one's eyes, one need only look at German taste, at German arts and mores: what peasant-like indifference to "taste"! How the noblest and meanest stand side by side! How disorderly and rich the entire household economy of this psyche! The German "lugs" his psyche; he "lugs" everything that he experiences. He digests his events poorly; he is never "done" with them. German profundity is often only a heavy sluggish digestive system. And as all chronic invalids, all dyspeptics, have a love for comfort, so the German loves "open-ness," "true blueness." How *comfortable* it is to be open and faithful. It is perhaps the most dangerous and happily chosen disguise, nowadays, which the German knows how to put on: the friendly-familiar, the accommodating showing of one's hand, this German candor. It is his proper Mephistophelean art; he could go "far" with it. The German lets himself go and looks at you with his true blue empty German eyes —and immediately any foreigner mistakes him for

GERMANS ARE CUNNING BASTARDS.

his night-gown. I meant to say that whatever German profundity may claim to be, we shall among ourselves permit ourselves to laugh at it. But we should do well to hold its appearance and good name in honor, henceforth as before, and not sell our old reputation as the people of depth too cheaply for Prussian "smartness" and Berlin wit and sand. It is clever of a people to make and to let themselves be taken for deep, clumsy, good-natured, candid, and un-clever. In fact it might even be—deep! And finally: one should do honor to one's name; not for nothing are we called the *tiusche*[1] nation, the *Täusche*-nation.

### 245.

The "good old times" have gone; they sang themselves out in Mozart. How happy *we* that his Rococo still speaks to us, that his "polite society," his tender yearning, his child-like delight in things Chinese and Arabesque, his courtesy of the heart, his longing for delicacy, amour, the dance, the smile-through-tears, his faith in the South, can still appeal to *something left* in us! Alas, some day it will all be gone—but who can doubt that our understanding and taste for Beethoven will go even sooner! Beethoven, after all, was only the echo of a style-transition, a style-break, and *not*, like Mozart, the echo of a great European taste that had lasted for centuries. Beethoven is the intermediate event between an old hollow psyche which forever crumbles and a new over-young psyche which forever *comes;* spread over his music is that

---

[1]  Nietzsche puns on "tiusch" (Old High German form of "deutsche")—German, and "täuschen"—to deceive. *Translator.*

twilight of everlasting losing and everlasting explor-
ing, hoping; the same light in which Europe lay
bathed when it was dreaming with Rousseau, dancing
around the freedom-tree of the Revolution, and
finally almost worshipping Napoleon. But how
quickly just that feeling fades, how difficult it is even
today to know about that feeling; how strange the
language of Rousseau, Schiller, Shelley, Byron sounds
to our ears, the language of all those combined, in
whom the common fate of Europe found its expression, the language which Beethoven knew how to
sing! Whatever German music came after him belongs to Romanticism; historically speaking, that is,
to an even shorter, even more fleeting and superficial
movement than that great *entr'acte,* that transition of
Europe from Rousseau to Napoleon to the advent
of democracy. There is Weber, but what do we
care about *Freischütz* and *Oberon* today? Or about
Marschner's *Hans Heiling* and *Vampyr?* Or even
about Wagner's *Tannhäuser.* That is played out, even
if not quite forgotten, music. The entire music of Romanticism was not distinguished enough, anyway, not
music enough, to maintain itself anywhere other than
in the theatre and before the masses; from the very
beginning it was a second-rate music which was not
taken seriously by real musicians. Felix Mendelssohn
is an exception, that halcyon master who, for the
sake of his slighter, purer, happier soul, was quickly
honored and equally quickly forgotten. He was a
lovely *episode* in German music. So far as Robert
Schumann is concerned, who took things seriously
and was himself taken seriously right from the start
(he is the last who founded a school), must we not
admit today that it is a good thing, a relief, a liberation, that this very Romanticism of Schumann is

surmounted? Schumann—escaping to the "Saxon Switzerland" [2] of his soul, half Werther, half Jean Paul, certainly not like Beethoven, nor like Byron—his Manfred-music is a mistake and a misunderstanding of Byron to the point of injustice—Schumann with his taste which was essentially a *petty* taste (a dangerous, among Germans doubly dangerous, inclination toward quiet lyricism and alcoholism of the emotions), constantly stepping aside, shyly withdrawing, a noble weakling wallowing in utterly anonymous bliss and pain, a sort of girl, a *noli me tangere* from the start: this Schumann was merely a *German* musical event, no longer a European one as Beethoven had been, as Mozart had been even more. In Schumann the greatest danger threatened German music, the danger that it would lose its *voice for the European psyche* and descend into mere patriotic drivel.

*GERMANNESS IS GOOD ONLY SO LONG AS IT IS EUROPEAN*

## 246.

What a torture German books are for someone who has the *third* ear! How unwillingly he stands besides the slowly revolving swamp of tones without tune, rhythms without dance, that the Germans call a "book." Not to speak of the Germans who *read* books! How lazily, unwillingly, badly, they read. How many Germans know or insist on knowing that there is art in every good sentence, an art that wants to be intuited if the sentence is to be understood. Misunderstand its tempo, for instance, and the whole sentence is misunderstood. To have no doubt regarding the rhythmically decisive syllables, to feel the

---

[2] Saxon Switzerland is a group of hills in the German province of Saxony. They are not very alpine in character; hence the reference is ironic. *Tr.*

breaking of too rigid a symmetry as intentional, and as a charm, to yield a subtle, patient ear to every *staccato*, every *rubato*, to guess the sense in the sequence of vowels and diphthongs, to see how delicately and richly they take on color from their surroundings: who among book-reading Germans has enough good will to recognize such duties and demands, who could listen to so much art and intention in language? They simply "have no ear for it," and so the strongest stylistic contrasts are not heard; the subtlest artistry is *wasted* as though on the deaf. —These were my thoughts when I noticed them clumsily and unknowingly confuse two masters of the art of prose. One of them dripped his words hesitantly and cold, as though from the ceiling of a damp cave: he was counting on their dull echoing plop. The other was handling his language like a flexible foil, feeling from his arm right down to his toe the dangerous bliss of the quivering razor-sharp blade, which is eager to bite, hiss, cut. . . .

## 247.

How little German style has to do with sound and hearing is shown by the fact that our good musicians, of all people, write poorly. The German does not read aloud; he reads not with the ear but merely with the eye; his ears he has put away in his desk drawer. When ancient man read—which happened rarely—he read aloud to himself, in a loud voice. If anyone read silently, everyone secretly wondered why. In a loud voice: that means with all the swellings, inflections, and variations of key and changes of tempo in which the ancient *public* world delighted. The laws for a written style were the same as the laws for a spoken style, and its laws depended in part on the astonishing development, the refined needs of the ear and the larynx, in part on the strength, endurance, and might of the ancient lungs. A period in the classical sense is above all a physiological whole, something that is enclosed by a single breath. Such periods as one finds in Demosthenes and Cicero, twice swelling, twice descending, all within the same breath: such periods were special treats for classical men, who could appreciate their virtue, the rarity and difficulty of their performance, from their own training. *We* don't really have a right to the *great* periods, we modern men, short of breath as we are in every sense. Those ancients were all dilettantes in speaking, hence connoisseurs, hence critics. Thus they drove their orators to extreme skill. In the same way during the last century, when all Italian men and women could sing, virtuosity in singing (and the art of melody along with it) reached a high peak. But in Germany (short of the most recent times when a sort of tribunal rhetoric is shyly and awkwardly lifting its young wings) there has been only one species of public and *roughly* artistic speech: that from the pulpit. Only the preacher in Germany knew what a syllable, what a word weighs, how a sentence strikes, jumps, falls, runs, and runs out; only the preacher had a conscience in his ears, and often enough a bad conscience, for there are plenty of reasons why a German attains proficiency in speech only rarely, and almost always too late. The masterpiece of German prose is therefore, fairly enough, the masterpiece of their greatest preacher. The *Bible* is still the best German book. Compared with Luther's Bible, almost everything else is merely "literature," a something which did not grow in Germany and hence never rooted in German hearts as the Bible did.

*IF HITLER'S IMMIGRATION, THE WORLD SHOULD ABORT.*

### 248.

There are two types of genius: one which above all impregnates and wants to impregnate; another which likes to be impregnated and gives birth. Likewise among the gifted nations there are those whose lot is the female problem of pregnancy, and the secret task of forming, maturing, perfecting—the Greeks, for example, were such a people, likewise the French—and others who must impregnate and become the cause of new orders of life—like the Jews, the Romans, and—let us ask modestly—the Germans perhaps? They are peoples who are tormented and enchanted by unknown fevers; irresistably they are forced to step outside of themselves; they love and lust after foreign races (those who will let themselves be impregnated); at the same time they are domineering like anything which knows that it is full of generative power and hence "the grace of God." These two types of genius seek each other like man and wife, but they also misunderstand each other—like man and wife.

### 249.

Each nation has its own "Tartuffery" and calls it its virtue. One does not know the best in oneself; one cannot know it.

### 250.

What does Europe owe the Jews? Many things, good and bad, but above all one thing that is among the best and the worst at the same time: the high style in morality, the frightfulness and majesty of

*SLAVE MORALITY BUT PRAISES TENACITY.*

infinite demands, infinite interpretations, the whole
romanticism and sublimity of moral problematics—
hence the most attractive, most insidious, most select
part of those colorplays and seductions to life in
whose after-glow the sky of European culture, its
evening sky, is today glowing—perhaps dying away.
We artists among the spectators and philosophers are
grateful for this to the Jews.

*PURSUIT OF MESSIAH ? MORALITY.*

### 251.

A nation which suffers—which wants to suffer—
from a case of nationalistic nerves and political ambitions must bargain on being subject to some cloud-
ing and disturbance of the mind, in short, some
small attacks of stupidity. The Germans of today,
for example, are afflicted now by the anti-French
stupidity, now by the anti-Semitic, now the anti-
Polish; then again by the Christian-Romantic disturbance, the Wagnerian, the Teutonic, the Prussian
(just look at those poor historians, those Sybel's and
Treitschke's with their heavily bandaged heads!), and
whatever else these small fogginesses of the German
mind and conscience may be called. I hope I shall
be forgiven if I too, during a brief reckless sojourn
in this infected territory, did not remain entirely free
from the disease; if I too, like everybody else, begin
to have thoughts about things which are none of my
business—the first symptom of political infection.
About the Jews, for example: listen. I have never yet
met a German who liked Jews. No matter how absolutely the cautious and the politically-minded reject
anti-Semitism as such, their caution and political consideration is never directed against the nature of the
sentiment itself, but only against its dangerous excess,
and particularly against the tedious and shameful ex-

pressions of such excess. We must not be deceived about this. That Germany has more than *enough* Jews, that the German stomach and blood find it difficult (and will do so for a long time to come) to absorb this amount of Jewry (as Italians, Frenchmen and Englishmen have done, with their stronger digestive powers): this is the plain declaration and expression of a general instinct to which one must listen and upon which one must act. "Let no new Jews in —close the doors against the East, in particular, including Austria": such is the instinct of a people whose character is still so weak and vague that it could easily be smudged out, even altogether wiped out, by a stronger race. And the Jews are beyond doubt the strongest, toughest and purest race now living in Europe; they know how to assert themselves in the midst of the worst possible conditions (better, in fact, than under more favorable ones). That they can do this is due to certain virtues of theirs, virtues which others would like to label as vices nowadays. Above all, due to their resolute faith, which need not be ashamed before "modern ideas," they change, *when* they change, in much the same fashion in which the Russian Empire makes its conquests (an Empire which has lots of time and is not of yesterday): according to the principle of "As slowly as possible." A thinker with the future of Europe on his conscience, will count on the Jews, in all his calculations for the future, just as he counts on the Russians. They are the most certain and most probable factors, for the time being, in the great game and struggle of powers. That which is called a nation in Europe today (more a *res facta* than *nata*[3]

---

[3] Thing made rather than born.

JEWS COULD & WILL TAKE OVER NOT SO PERENNIAL GERMANY.

and at times indistinguishable from a *res ficta et picta*)[4] is in each case something that is in process, something young and easily altered. By no means is it a race, much less such an *aere perennius* as the Jewish type. The so-called nations should really beware of any hot-headed rivalry and hostility among themselves. That the Jews could right now have the ascendency, in fact literally the supremacy, over Europe if they wanted it, or if they were forced to take it as the anti-Semites seem to be after, is certain. It is equally certain that the Jews are *not* working toward this end, nor making plans for it. For the time being they want and desire, even with some insistence, to be absorbed; they thirst to be settled, somewhere where they are allowed and respected, to make an end to their nomadic life, to the "Wandering Jew." And the others should note this feature, this impulse (which is perhaps in itself a withdrawing of the Jewish instincts) and meet it half way. To this end it would be useful and just to banish from the country the anti-Semitic cry-babies. The Jews should be met half way, with caution, with selectivity, approximately as the British aristocracy has done it. It is obvious that the stronger and more stable types among the modern Germans could do this with the least precariousness—for example the officers of the Prussian landed gentry. It would be interesting from many points of view to see whether the hereditary art of command and obedience (for which the region in question is classical) could not be added to and interbred with the genius for finance and patience (and above all some intellectuality—for utter lack of which this same region is notorious). But at this

[4] Fictitious and pictured (i.e. twice removed from reality).

point it is proper to break off my cheerful Germanic twaddle, my national-holiday speech—for I am now touching upon my *serious* problem: the European problem as I understand it: the breeding of a new caste which is to rule Europe.

*THATS ? HE IS TYPING THESE NATIONALITIES*

### 252.

These Englishmen: they are not a philosophical race. Bacon constitutes a downright *attack* on the philosophic spirit; Hobbes, Hume and Locke were a depreciation, a devaluation of the concept "philosopher" for more than a century. It was *against* Hume that Kant rose and elevated himself; it was Locke of whom Schelling had a *right* to say "je méprise Locke." In their struggle against the English-mechanistic world-idiotizing, Hegel and Schopenhauer (together with Goethe) were of one mind; those two hostile brother geniuses in philosophy who spread out toward opposite poles of the German spirit and were therefore unjust to one another as only brothers can be. What England lacks and has always lacked was well enough known by that ham actor and rhetorician, that insipid muddle-head Carlyle. And he sought to hide it beneath passionate grimaces, but he knew that it was true of himself as well. What is lacking is genuine *power* of intellect, genuine *depth* of intellectual perception, in short—philosophy. It is characteristic of such an unphilosophical race that they cling firmly to Christianity; they *need* its discipline to become "moralized," to become "humanized." The Englishman, more depressed, more sensual, stronger in willpower, and more brutal than the German, is for this reason, because he is the more common of the two, more pious; he simply *needs* Christianity more. For keen

*THE ENGLISH HAVE NEVER BEEN STRONG—*
*CHRISTIANS — STRONGER THAN MOST —*
*A CHRISTIANS — SLAVES NOT THEIR HISTORY*
*THEY ARE SLAVES NOT THEIR HISTORY*

noses even the Christianity of England has a typically British odor of spleen and alcoholic excess. No wonder it is used as a cure. It is a case of the subtler poison as antidote for the grosser; among boorish nations a subtle poisoning is indeed progress, a step toward intellectualization. British boorishness and peasant-like earnestness are most easily endured in the guise of Christian pantomime, praying and psalm-singing—or better, they are properly interpreted or re-interpreted. In that cattleherd of alcoholics and eccentrics whom Methodism used to teach how to make moral "moo's," and who learn it nowadays from the Salvation Army, a penitential fit may really constitute the comparatively highest attainable level of "humane" achievement: that much must be admitted. But what is insulting in even the most human Englishman is his lack of music, to speak metaphorically (and also literally!). There is no rhythm, no dance, in the motions of his soul or his body. He doesn't even have a desire for rhythm and dance, for "music." Listen to him speak; look at the most beautiful Englishwomen *walk* (there are no more beautiful doves and swans in any country on earth); finally listen to them sing! But I am asking too much—

## 253.

There are truths which are best recognized by mediocre intellects because they are most suited to them; there are truths which possess charm and seductive powers for mediocre spirits only. We come to this somewhat unpleasant conclusion when we see the intellect of respectable but mediocre Englishmen (I name Darwin, John Stuart Mill and Herbert Spencer) making their weight felt upon the middling regions of European taste. Indeed, who would deny the usefulness of the fact that such minds are at times preponderant! It would be an error to consider highly developed superior and independent minds as especially capable for determining and collecting many small common facts, or prodding them into conclusions. They are the exception, and as such in no favorable position to deal with the "rule." In the end, they have more to do than merely know—they have to *be* something new, to *signify* something new, to *represent* new values. The chasm between knowing and being able to do is perhaps greater and more uncanny than one might think. He who can *do* things in high style, the creator, may possibly have to be someone who is unknowing—whereas on the other hand a certain narrowness, barrenness and diligent carefulness, in short, something British, may be well disposed to scientific discoveries of the Darwinian type. Let us not forget that we already owe to Englishmen a total depression of the European spirit, brought about by their profound mediocrity. What we now call "modern ideas" or "eighteenth century ideas" or "French ideas"—everything, in other words, against which the German spirit has risen in deep disgust—was of English origin. There can be no doubt about it. The French were merely the apes and actors of these ideas; they were also the best soldiers defending them and alas, their first and most thoroughgoing *victims;* for ultimately the *âme française* has become so skinny and emaciated from its damnable anglomania of "modern ideas," that one is almost incredulous today when one remembers the French sixteenth and seventeenth centuries, their deep, passionate power, and their creative distinction. But one must hang on to this proposition of historical justice with one's teeth, defending it against the moment and against all apparent evidence: European *noblesse*— of feeling, taste, mores, in short in every superior sense—is the work and invention of *France;* European commonness, the plebeianism of modern ideas, belongs to England.

254.

*HOW CAN HE TYPE THESE NATIONS.? INDIVIDUALISM IS THE KEY.*

Even today France is still the seat of the most intellectual and sophisticated culture of Europe, and the academy of taste, but—one must know where to find the "France of taste." Whoever is part of it is keeping under cover; it is probably a small number among whom it lives and has its being. Besides, they may be people who are not standing on very sturdy legs; fatalists in part, depressed individuals, sick ones, persons partly over-indulged, partly over-sophisticated —all sorts of people who have the *pride* to conceal themselves. One thing they all have in common: they stop up their ears before the raging stupidity and the noisy squabble of the democratic bourgeoisie. In the foreground, to be sure, there wallows today an idiotized and coarsened France. (The other day they celebrated a veritable orgy of bad taste and self-admiration in their funeral for Victor Hugo.) And something else the concealed France has in common: the good will to defend itself against intellectual Germanization—and an even better incapacity to do this. Schopenhauer is perhaps even today more at home in this France of the spirit, which is also the France of Pessimism, than he ever was in Germany; not to mention Heinrich Heine who has long since gone over into the flesh and blood of the more subtle and demanding Parisian lyricists, or of Hegel who

*SO CULTIVATED.*

*VULGAR GERMAN TASTE + ENGLISH MORALITY.*

today in the form of Taine (that is the *foremost* living historian) exerts an almost tyrannical influence. But as regards Richard Wagner, the more French music learns to shape itself to the real needs of the *âme moderne,* the more there will be of "Wagnerization" —one may safely predict. It is being done already. Nonetheless there are three things which the French can point to with pride even today as their heritage and their own, and as the indelible sign of an ancient cultural supremacy over Europe, in spite of all voluntary and involuntary Germanization and plebeianization of taste. The first is that they are capable of artistic passions, of devotion to "form," for which the expression *l'art pour l'art* has been coined in addition to thousands of others. Something like it has not been lacking in France for three centuries. Again and again, due to their respect for the "small number," a sort of chamber music of literature has been made possible. One looks in vain for anything like it in the rest of Europe. The second thing on which the French can ground their superiority over Europe is their ancient, complex *moralistic* culture which lets us find, even in the small *romanciers* of the newspapers and the chance *boulevardiers de Paris* a high average level of psychological sensitiveness and inquisitiveness such as one could hardly imagine (much less demonstrate!) in Germany. The Germans would need several centuries of moralistic work to reach this level, centuries which France did not hesitate to spend. Whoever calls the Germans naïve for this reason praises them for a fault. (As the opposite to German inexperience with and innocence of psychological delights—not too far removed as they are from the boring quality of German intercourse— and as the most successful expression of genuinely

French inquisitiveness and inventiveness in this domain of delicate thrills, I point to Henri Beyle, that remarkable anticipatory and advanced individual who, with Napoleonic speed, ran through *his* Europe, through several centuries of the European psyche, sniffing it out and discovering it. It took two generations to even approximately *catch up* with him, merely to follow in his footsteps by way of guessing the answer to some of the riddles which tortured and charmed him—Henri Beyle, that strange Epicurean and question-mark man, that last great French psychologist.) France has a third claim to supremacy: in the French nature there is a halfway successful synthesis of North and South. This enables them to comprehend things and do things which an Englishman could never comprehend. The French temperament, turned alternately toward and away from the South, their Provençal and Ligurian blood which from time to time spills over, saves them from the gruesome Nordic grey-on-grey, from the sunless conceptual skeleton and anemia, from the whole taste-disease that we Germans suffer from, the same disease which just at present has firmly prescribed for itself "blood and iron," i.e. "high politics." (A dangerous healing art: it bids me wait and see but scarcely hope.) Even today there is in France a pre-understanding and an acceptance of those rare and rarely satisfied men who are too extensive to find satisfaction in patriotic drivel of any sort. They know how to love the South in the North, the North in the South. They are the born "Medi-terraneans," the "good Europeans." *Bizet* has composed their music for them: Bizet, that last genius who saw a new beauty and seduction, who discovered a piece of the *South for Music.*

### 255.

I consider several precautions necessary for dealing with German music. Assuming anyone loves the South as I love it, as a high academy for convalescence in things intellectual as well as sensual, as a boundless sunniness and sun-transfiguration that floods an autonomous existence which believes in itself: such a man learns to beware somewhat of German music because it sets him back, both in his taste and in his health. If such a Southerner (not by birth but by faith) should dream of the future of music, he must dream of the liberation of music from the North; he must have in his ears the prelude to a deeper, mightier, perhaps more evil and more mysterious music; a supra-German music which would not die away or fade or pale before the sight of the blue voluptuous sea or the mediterranean clarity of the sky, as does all German music; which would maintain its individuality even before the brown sunsets of the desert; whose soul was related to the palm tree and knew how to roam and be at home among great beautiful lonely cats of prey.—I could imagine a music whose rarest charm would be that it no longer knew anything of good and evil, except that some fleeting sailor's nostalgia, some slight golden shadows and tender regret ran over it now and then. I could imagine an art which saw, at a great distance, the colors of a sinking, almost incomprehensible *moral* world, sending its last gleams into space, an art which would be hospitable and deep enough to receive such last-minute refugees.

### 256.

Thanks to the pathological estrangement which the

insanity of "nationality" has placed, and still places, between the nations of Europe; thanks, likewise to the short-sighted and nimble-fingered politicians who are in power today, with the help of this nonsense, and who do not have a notion how much their politics can only be an interlude; thanks to all this and more which is quite unspeakable today, the most obvious and unambiguous signs that *Europe wishes to become One* are today either overlooked or arbitrarily and mendaciously misinterpreted. The genuine main direction, the mysterious psychic activity, of all the deeper and more extensive men of this century was to prepare the way to that new synthesis, to anticipate experimentally the European of the future. Only in their surface activity or in their weaker hours, in old age perhaps, did they belong to the "fatherlands." Only when they took a rest from themselves did they become "patriots." I am thinking of men such as Napoleon, Goethe, Beethoven, Stendhal, Heine, and Schopenhauer; no one should take it amiss if I count Richard Wagner among them as well, for one must not be misled by Wagner's own misunderstanding of himself. Geniuses of his type seldom have the right to understand themselves correctly. Still more one must discount the unseemly noise with which France nowadays blocks and defends itself against Wagner. The fact remains that *late French Romanticism* of the forties and Richard Wagner belong closely and intimately one to the other. They are related, basically related, in all the heights and depths of their needs: it is Europe, One Europe, whose soul pushes outward and upward through all their manifold and impetuous art. But where to? Into a new light? Toward a new sun? Still, who could express precisely what all these masters of new expressive forms could not them-

STRENGTH IN BARBARISM

selves express plainly? One thing is certain: the same storm and stress tortured them all; these last great seekers sought in the same way! All of them, these first artists of a universal literary culture, all of them are dominated by literature—down to their eyes and ears; most of them were themselves writers, poets, mediators and minglers of the arts and the senses (as a musician, Wagner is a painter; as a poet he is a musician; as an artist as such, he is an actor). All of them are fanatics of *expression* at any cost. I especially mention Delacroix, Wagner's closest relative. All of them were great discoverers in the realm of the sublime, also of the ugly and the horrifying; even greater discoverers of new effects, of advertising, of shop-window art. All of them had talents far surpassing their genius; they were thoroughgoing virtuosos, with uncanny entry into anything seductive, alluring, compelling, and upsetting. They were born enemies of logic and straight lines, greedy for things foreign, for the exotic, the monstrous, the crooked, the self-contradictory. As men, every one of them was a Tantalus of the will, a late-come plebeian who knew he was incapable of a distinguished tempo, a *lento*, in either life or art—think of Balzac for example! They were unbridled workers, almost self-destroyers through work; antinomists and rebels in behavior, ambitious and insatiable without balance or ability to enjoy themselves. And all of them in the end broke up and sank down before the Christian cross (which was proper enough; for who of them was deep and original enough for a philosophy of the Anti-Christ?). On the whole they were a recklessly daring, magnificently violent, high-flying type of superior men, made to sweep others off their feet.

They had to teach their century—the century of the *masses*—the meaning of "superior man." . . . Let the German friends of Richard Wagner consider whether there is anything plainly German in Wagnerian art, or whether it isn't rather its distinction that it blows from supra-German sources and impulses. And let them not underrate how indispensable Paris was for the development of a type such as Wagner's. The depths of his instincts bade him demand Paris at just the decisive time; and the whole manner of his performance, his self-styled apostolate, could only be perfected within the orbit of the French socialist model. Perhaps it will be found to the honor of Richard Wagner's German nature, upon delicate comparative study, that he did everything harder, more recklessly, more powerfully and to a higher point than a nineteenth century Frenchman could have done, thanks to the fact that we Germans are still closer to barbarism than the French. Perhaps, in fact, the most noteworthy thing that Wagner created will be not only today but forever inaccessible, unimaginable, and inimitable to the whole ancient Latin race: I mean the figure of Siegfried, that *very free* human being, who may indeed be by far too free, too hard, cheerful, healthy, and anti-Catholic for the taste of old and hollow cultivated nations. This anti-romantic Siegfried may even be a sin against Romanticism—but never mind! Wagner has more than atoned for this sin in the depressed days of his old age, when with his unique religious vehemence, and anticipating a taste which has since become political, he began to preach if not to go *the way to Rome*. Lest my last words should be misunderstood, I shall reveal with the aid of a few

healthy rhymes to less delicate ears, too, what I want:
what I want and have *against* the "latter-day Wagner"
and his *Parsifal* music.

You call this German?
Does German heart shriek out this sultry grating?
Does German flesh writhe in self-mutilating?
German this priestly hand-on-laying?
This incense-sniffling tickle-playing?
German this halting, faltering, tangling,
This shilly-shallying ding-dong-dangling?
This ogling of nuns, this angelus-jingling,
This whole paroxysmal false heaven-tingling?
—-You call this German?
You're only at the door. Consider what comes next!
For what you hear is Rome—Rome's faith without
  the text.

# NINTH ARTICLE

## WHAT DOES "DISTINGUISH" MEAN?

### 257.

Every heightening of the type "man" hitherto has been the work of an aristocratic society—and thus it will always be; a society which believes in a long ladder of rank order and value differences in men, which needs slavery in some sense. Without the *pathos of distance* as it grows out of the deep-seated differences of caste, out of the constant view, the downward view, that the ruling caste gets of its subordinates and tools, out of its equally constant exercise in obeying and commanding, in keeping apart and keeping a distance—without this pathos of distance there could not grow that other more mysterious pathos, that longing for ever greater distances within the soul itself, the evolving of ever higher, rarer, more spacious, more widely arched, more comprehensive states—in short: the heightening of the type "man," the continued "self-mastery of man," to take a moral formula in a supra-moral sense. To be sure, we must not yield to humanitarian self-deception about the history of the origins of an aristocratic society (in other words, the presuppositions for the heightening of the type "man"): the truth is hard. Let us tell ourselves without indulging ourselves how every superior culture on earth got its *start!* Men whose nature was still natural, barbarians in every frightful sense of the word, men of prey, men still in possession of unbroken strength of will and power-drives—such men threw themselves upon weaker, better-behaved, more peaceable races, possibly those engaged in commerce or cattle-raising, or else upon old hollow cultures in which the last life powers were flickering away in flashing fireworks of intellect and corruption. The distinguished caste in the beginning was always the barbarian caste; their superiority lay not primarily in their physical but in their psychic power; they were more whole as human beings (which on every level also means "more whole as beasts").

### 258.

Corruption is the expression of the fact that there is anarchy which threatens to spread among the instincts, and that the basic structure of the passions, called "life," has been shaken. Types of corruption are radically different from one another, depending on the life-structure in which they show up. When for example an aristocracy, such as that of France at the start of the Revolution, throws away its privileges with a sublime nausea, and sacrifices itself to an extravagance of its moral feelings, that is corruption. It was really only the final act of that century-long corruption in the course of which the aristocracy yielded step by step its ruling prerogatives and lowered itself until it was a *function* of royalty (and in the very end merely its ornament and crowning glory). But the essential nature of a good and healthy aristocracy is that it does *not* feel it is a function (whether of royalty or of the community) but its meaning, its highest justification. Therefore it accepts with a clear conscience the sacrifice of an enormous number of men who must *for the sake of the aristocracy* be suppressed and reduced to incomplete human beings, to slaves, to tools. It must be aristocracy's basic belief that society exists *not* for the sake of society, but only as the foundation, the skeleton structure, by means of which a select kind of creature can raise itself to a higher task, a higher level of *being*—like those sun-seeking climbing plants in Java, called *Sipo Matador,* which cling to an oak so long and so often until finally they unfold their crowns in the open air, displaying their bliss high above the oak but supported by it.

## 259.

To refrain from wounding, violating, and exploiting one another, to acknowledge another's will as equal to one's own: this can become proper behavior, in a certain coarse sense, between individuals when the conditions for making it possible obtain (namely the factual similarity of the individuals as to power and standards of value, and their co-existence in one greater body). But as soon as one wants to extend this principle, to make it the *basic principle of society,* it shows itself for what it is: the will to negate life, the principle of dissolution and decay. Here one must think radically to the very roots of things and ward off all weakness of sensibility. Life itself is essential assimilation, injury, violation of the foreign and the weaker, suppression, hardness, the forcing of one's own forms upon something else, ingestion and—at least in its mildest form—exploitation. But why should we always use such words which were coined from time immemorial to reveal a calumniatory intention? Even that body to which we referred, the body within which individuals may treat each other with equality (and it is so in any healthy aristocracy) —even this body itself, if it is alive and not dying off, must do to other bodies all the things from which its members refrain; it will have to be the will to power incarnate; it will have to want to grow, to branch out, to draw others into itself, to gain supremacy. And not because it is moral or immoral in any sense but because it is *alive,* and because life simply *is* will to power. But there is no point at which the common consciousness in Europe today is less willing to lean than just here; everywhere today, and even in the guise of science, there is grandiose talk about future social conditions where there is to be no more "exploitation." To my ears that sounds as though they promised to invent a kind of life that would refrain from all the organic functions. "Exploitation" is not a part of a vicious or imperfect or primitive society: it belongs to the *nature* of living things, it is a basic organic function, a consequence of the will to power which is the will to life. Admitted that this is a novelty as a theory—as a reality it is the *basic fact* underlying all history. Let us be honest with ourselves at least this far!

## 260.

Wandering through the many fine and coarse moralities which have hitherto ruled on earth, as well as those which still rule, I found certain features regularly occurring together and bound up with one another. Finally they revealed two basic types to me, and a basic difference leaped to my eye. There is *master-morality* and *slave-morality:* I add immediately that in all higher and mixed cultures there are also attempts at a mediation between these two, and even more frequently a mix-up of them and a mutual misunderstanding; at times in fact a relentless juxtaposition even within the psyche of a single individual. The moral value-differentiations arose either among a ruling type which was pleasantly conscious of its difference from the ruled—or else among the ruled, the slaves and dependents of all kinds. In the first case, when the rulers determine the concept "good," it is the elevated and proud conditions of the psyche which are felt to be what excels and determines the order of rank. The distinguished human being divorces himself from the being in whom the opposite of such elevated and proud conditions is expressed. He despises them. One may note immediately that in the first type of morality the antithesis "good vs. bad" means "distinguished vs. despicable"; the antithesis "good vs. evil" has a different origin. What is despised is the coward, the timid man, and the petty man, he who thinks in terms of narrow utility; likewise the suspicious man with his cowed look, the one who humiliates himself, the dog-type who lets himself be mistreated, the begging flatterer, and above all the liar: it is the basic faith of all aristocrats that the common people are liars. "We truthful ones" the nobles called themselves in ancient Greece. It is obvious that the moral value-characteristics are at first applied to *people* and only later, in a transferred sense, to *acts*. This is why it is a sad mistake when moral historians begin with questions like "Why was the compassionate act praised?" The distinguished type of human being feels *himself* as value-determining; he does not need to be ratified; he judges that "which is harmful to me is harmful as such"; he knows that *he* is the something which gives honor to objects; he *creates values*. This type honors everything he knows about himself; his morality is self-glorification. In the foreground is the feeling of fullness, of power that would flow forth, the bliss of high tension, the consciousness of riches which would like to give and lavish. The distinguished man, too,

helps the unhappy, but not—at least not mainly—
from compassion, but more from an internal pressure that has been built up by an excess of power.
The distinguished man honors himself in the mighty,
including those who have power over themselves;
those who know when to talk and when to keep
silent; those who take delight in being rigorous and
hard with themselves and who have respect for anything rigorous and hard. "Wotan placed a hard heart
in my breast," says an old Scandinavian saga: this
is the proper poetic expression for the soul of a proud
Viking. Such a type of man is proud *not* to have
been made for compassion; hence the hero of the
saga adds a warning: "Whoever has not a hard heart
when young will never get it at all." Distinguished
and courageous men with such thoughts are at the
opposite end from that morality which sees the
characteristic function of morality in pity or in doing
for others or *désintéressement*. Belief in oneself,
pride in oneself, basic hostility and irony against "self-
lessness" is as sure a part of distinguished morality as
an easy disdain and cautious attitude toward the
fellow-feelings and the "warm heart." It is the powerful men who *understand* how to accord honor: that
is their art, the domain of their invention. Profound
respect for old age and for origins: their whole law
stands on this twofold respect. Faith in and prepos-
session for one's ancestors and prejudice against the
future ones is typical of the morality of the powerful. Contrariwise, when men of "modern ideas" believe almost instinctively in "progress" and in "the
future" and have less and less respect for the old,
that alone reveals clearly enough the undistinguished
origin of their "ideas." But the point at which the
morality of rulers is most foreign to current taste

and most painstakingly strict in principle is this: one has duties only toward one's equals; toward beings of a lower rank, toward everything foreign to one, one may act as one sees fit, "as one's heart dictates"—in any event, "beyond good and evil." The ability and the duty to sustain enduring gratitude and enduring vengefulness—both only toward one's equals; subtlety in requital and retaliation; a subtly refined concept of friendship; a certain need to have enemies (as outlets for the passions: envy, quarrelsomeness and wantonness—basically, in order to be capable of being a good *friend):* all these are typical marks of the distinguished type of morality which, as I have indicated, is not the morality of "modern ideas" and hence is difficult today to empathize with, and equally difficult to dig out and uncover.—The situation is different with the second type of morality, the slave morality. Assuming that the violated ones, the oppressed, the suffering, the unfree, those who are uncertain and tired of themselves—assuming that they moralize: What will they have in common in their moral evaluations? Probably a pessimistic suspiciousness against the whole situation of mankind will appear; perhaps a judgment against mankind together with its position. The eye of the slave looks unfavorably upon the virtues of the powerful; he *subtly* mistrusts all the "good" that the others honor —he would like to persuade himself that even their happiness is not real. Conversely, those qualities are emphasized and illuminated which serve to make existence easier for the sufferers: here compassion, the complaisant helping hand, the warm heart, patience, diligence, humility and friendliness are honored, for these are the useful qualities and almost the only means for enduring the pressure of existence.

Slave-morality is essentially a utility-morality. Here is the cornerstone for the origin of that famous Antithesis "good vs. evil." Power and dangerousness, a certain frightfulness, subtlety and strength which do not permit of despisal, are felt to belong to evil. Hence according to slave morality, the "evil" man inspires fear; according to master morality, the "good" man does and wants to, where as the "bad" man is felt to be despicable. The antithesis reaches its sharpest point when ultimately the "good" man within a slave morality becomes the logical target of a breath of disdain—however slight and well-meaning, because he is the *undangerous* element in his morality: good natured, easily deceived, perhaps a little stupid, *un bonhomme*. Whenever slave morality preponderates, language shows a tendency to reconcile the meanings of "good" and "dumb." A final basic distinction is that the longing for *freedom,* the instinct for happiness and the subtleties of the freedom-feelings belong as necessarily to slave morality as skill and enthusiasm for reverence, for devotion, is the regular symptom of an aristocratic manner of thinking and evaluating.—This enables us to understand easily why love *as passion* (our European specialty) must be of distinguished origin; we know it was invented by the Provençal knightly poets, those magnificent inventive men of *gai saber*[1]—to whom Europe owes so much, and almost itself.

## 261.

Vanity belongs among the things which are hardest for a distinguished man to comprehend; he is tempted

[1] Gay learning. Nietzsche used the phrase for the title of a previous work, *Die fröhliche Wissenschaft. Tr.*

to deny it where it is painfully obvious to another type of man. His problem is that he cannot imagine creatures who seek to stimulate a good opinion of themselves in others—an opinion which they do not share and hence do not "deserve"—and who then *believe* in that good opinion. To the distinguished man this seems partly such bad taste and lack of respect for oneself and partly so baroquely irrational that it is easier for him to think of vanity as an exceptional state and to doubt its presence in most cases where others see it. He will say, for example, "I can be wrong about my worth and yet demand that it be recognized by others in the terms in which I announce it"—this is not vanity, however, but conceit, or, more frequently, what is known as "humility" or "modesty." Or he can say, "I may rejoice in other people's opinion for many reasons: perhaps because I love and honor them and rejoice in any of their rejoicings; perhaps because their good opinion echoes and supports my own good opinion; perhaps because the good opinion of others, even when I do not share it, is useful to me or promises to be useful—but all this is not vanity either." The distinguished man has to compel himself, with the help of history, to realize that since time immemorial the common man in any dependent strata of mankind *was* only what he *was taken for.* He was not accustomed to pose values of his own, and he never estimated himself to be of any value other than that accorded him by his masters. (For it is the intrinsic *right of masters* to create values.) One may consider it the consequence of an enormous atavism that the ordinary man even today *waits* for an opinion of himself and then instinctively subordinates himself to it—by no means always a "good" opinion, however; just as likely a bad or an unfair one. (Think, for example, of the majority of self-ratings and self-underratings that pious women learn from their father confessors, and pious Christians in general from their church!) Thanks to the slow rise of the democratic order of things (which goes back to a mingling of master and slave) the originally distinguished and rare impulse to ascribe one's own value to oneself, to think well of oneself, is in fact more and more encouraged and spread out. But at all times it has working against it an older, broader, and more thoroughly imbedded tendency—and in the phenomenon of "vanity" this older tendency masters the new. The vain man is just as pleased with *every* good opinion about himself that he hears (quite aside from any utility and any truth or falseness involved) as he suffers from every bad opinion. For he subordinates himself to both; he *feels* himself dependent on them, out of that ancient instinct of dependency that breaks out in him.—It is the "slave" in the blood of the vain, a remainder of slave-like slyness (how much of the "slave" is still reactionary-active in women, for example!) that seeks to *seduce* others to have good opinions about him; it is likewise the slave who immediately falls down before those opinions just as though he had not called them forth.—To say it once more: vanity is an atavism.

## 262.

A species, a *type* originates, and grows firm and strong, in a long struggle with essentially constant but unfavorable conditions. Conversely, we know from the experience of breeders that species which get superabundant nourishment and generally more protection and care tend very strongly to variations in type; they are rich in miracles and monstrosities (including monstrous vices). Now let us look at an aristocratic community (an ancient Greek *polis,* for example, or Venice) as though it were a voluntary or involuntary institution for the purpose of breeding: there are men in it, intermingled and dependent on one another, who want to propagate their type, mostly because they *must,* or because they are in some terrible danger of being exterminated. Here all favoritism, all abundance, all protection is lacking with which variations are furthered; the species needs itself as a species, as something which can only assert itself and make itself last by means of hardness, monotony of form, and, in general, simplicity. For they are in constant battle with their neighbors or their subordinates who are rebelling or are threatening to rebel. All sorts of experience teaches them to which of their qualities in particular they owe their continuous existence, the whole line of their victories in spite of all gods and men. These qualities they call virtues; these virtues alone breed greatness into them. Aristocratic morality acts harshly; it wants hardness; it is intolerant—in the education of youth, in the disposition of woman, in marriage customs, in the relations between the generations, in the primitive laws (which are directed solely toward the ones who threaten to vary from the type). Aristocratic morality counts intolerance itself among the virtues, calling it "justice." A type with few but strong characteristics, a kind of rigorous warrior-like cleverly silent, closed off and reserved man (who, being such, has a very subtle sense for the charm and nuances of sociability) is in this fashion stabilized beyond the changes from generation to generation; the constant struggle with ever constant un-

favorable conditions, as I have said, is the reason
why a type becomes solid and hard. But finally some
day there arise favorable conditions; the enormous
tension slackens; perhaps there are no more enemies
among the neighbors; the means for living and even
for the enjoyment of life are suddenly superabundant. All at once the bond breaks, the compulsion
of the old discipline no longer feels itself as necessary, as determining men's very existence. If it wants
to endure beyond this point, it can do so only as a
form of *luxury,* as a *taste* for the archaic. Variety
(whether as variation into higher, subtler, rarer
forms, or as deterioration and monstrosity) suddenly
appears on the scene in great abundance and magnificence; the individual dares to individuate himself.
At these turning points of history there shows itself
juxtaposed and often completely entangled with one
another a magnificent, manifold, jungle-like growing
and striving, a sort of *tropical* tempo in rivalry of
development, and an enormous destruction and self-
destruction thanks to the egoisms violently opposed
to one another, exploding as it were, battling each
other for sun and light, unable to find any limitation,
any check, any considerateness within the morality
at their disposal. It was the morality itself which
had accumulated power to the point of enormity,
which had so dangerously tensed the bow: now, at
this moment, it is "outlived." The dangerous and
uncanny point has been reached where a greater,
more complex, more extensive life *lives beyond, out-
reaches,* the old morality. The "individual" stands
ready, needing a set of laws of his own, needing his
own skills and wiles for self-preservation, self-height-
ening, self-liberation. Nothing but new "wherefore's",
nothing but new "wherewith's," no longer any com-

munal formulas; a new alliance of misunderstanding
and mutual disrespect; decay, vice, and the most
superior desires gruesomely bound up with one another, the genius of the race welling up over all the
cornucopias of good and ill; a fateful simultaneity
of spring and autumn, full of new charms and misty
veils that adhere to the young, the still unexhausted,
unwearied perversion. Again there is danger, the
mother of morality—great danger—but this time dis-
placed onto the individual, onto the nearest and
dearest, onto the street, onto one's own child, one's
own heart, one's innermost and secret recesses of
wish and will: what will the morality philosophers
who emerge now have to preach? They discover,
these keen observers and Little Jack Horners, that
the end is rapidly approaching, that everything
around them is approaching ruin and making for
ruination, that nothing will last till the day after tomorrow except one type of man: the incurably
*mediocre*. Only the mediocre have prospects for
continuing and reproducing their kind; they are the
men of the future, the sole survivors. "Be like them!
Become mediocre!"—is now the sole morality that
makes sense, that finds ears to hear. But it is hard
to preach it, this morality of mediocrity! For it can
never admit what it is and what it wants. It must
talk about measure and dignity and duty and love
for one's neighbor—it will have trouble *hiding its
irony!*—

### 263.

There is an *instinct for rank* which is, more than
anything else, the sign of a *high* rank; there is a delight in nuances of reverence which reveals distinguished origin and habits. The subtlety, goodness,

and elevation of a soul is dangerously tested when something of first rank passes by it, without being guarded as yet by the shudders of authority from importunate touchings and grossness; something which goes along its way, unmarked, undiscovered, experimentally—perhaps intentionally—shrouded and disguised, like a living touchstone. Someone who makes it his task and exercise to probe souls will make use of this knowledge in many ways, in order to determine the ultimate value of a soul, its immovably inborn order of rank. He will test a soul for its *instinct of reverence. Différence engendre haine:* the meanness of some natures suddenly splashes up like dirty water when some holy vessel, some precious object out of a locked shrine, some book with the signs of high destiny imprinted upon it, is carried past them. Some, on the other hand, become involuntarily silent, hesitant of eye, quiet of gesture, and thereby express that their soul *feels* the proximity of an object worthy of deep reverence. The manner, on the whole, in which reverence for the *Bible* is still preserved in Europe is perhaps the best part of discipline and refinement of behavior that Europe owes to Christianity; such books of depth and ultimate significance need the protection of an external tyranny of authority, in order to gain those millenniums of *preservation* which are necessary to exhaust them and read all their riddles. Much is gained, when the feeling is finely bred into the masses (the flatheads and runny-guts of all sorts) that there are some things they may not touch; that there are sacred experiences in the presence of which they are to remove their shoes and keep their dirty hands to themselves: this is almost their highest possible approximation to humanity. Conversely, noth-

ing is so nauseating in the so-called cultured intellectuals, the believers in "modern ideas" as their lack
of shame, their complaisant impudence of eye and
hand with which they touch, lick, and finger everything. It is possible that among the common people,
on the lowest levels, particularly among peasants,
there is more relative distinction of taste and tactfulness of reverence today than among the newspaper-
reading *demi-monde* of the intellect, the educated
intellectuals.

### 264.

It cannot be erased from a man's psyche what his
ancestors liked best and did most; whether they were
diligent economizers, part and parcel of a desk or a
cash-box, modest and bourgeois in their desires and
modest also in their virtues; or whether they lived
from early till late accustomed to giving orders, fond
of rough entertainment—and of even rougher duties
and responsibilities besides; or finally whether they
at some time sacrificed old privileges of birth and
property in order to live wholly for their belief, their
"god," as men of an inexorable and delicate conscience which blushes at any mediation. It is simply
not possible for a man *not* to have in his body the
qualities and predilections of his parents and ancestors, no matter what appearances seem to be
against it. This is the problem of race. If one knows
something of the parents one can permit oneself
some conclusions about the child. A certain repulsive incontinence, a dog-in-the-manger enviousness,
a boorish desire to be always right (these three together having composed the genuine rabble-type at
all times)—such things must be transferred to the
child as surely as contaminated blood. With the help

of the best education and cultivation one will only manage to *deceive* others as to the child's heritage.—And what else do education and culture want today? In our very popularly-minded, i.e. rabble-minded times, education and culture *must* essentially be the art of deception—as to one's origin, one's inherited rabble in body and soul. An educator who today would preach truthfulness above all, who constantly admonished his charges to be "true," to be "natural —be what you are"—even such a virtuous and well-meaning ass would learn shortly to grasp that *furca* of Horace's, in order *naturam expellere*. With what result, however? "Rabble" *usque recurret.*—

### 265.

At the risk of displeasing innocent ears, I propose the following: Egoism belongs to the nature of a distinguished soul. I mean that immovable faith that other beings are by nature subordinate to a being such as "we are"; that they should sacrifice themselves to us. The distinguished soul accepts this fact of its egoism without any question mark, and also without any feeling that it is hard or oppressive or arbitrary; rather as something which may be founded in the basic law of all things. If it were to look for a name for its feeling, it would say, "This is justice itself." It admits, under certain circumstances which at first make it hesitate, that there are other souls who are its equals as to rights. As soon as it clarifies for itself this question of rank, it moves among its equals with the same sureness in modesty and delicate respect that it has toward itself, according to an inborn stellar mechanism which the stars understand well. It is a *further* aspect of its egoism, this subtlety and self-limitation in intercourse with its peers—

every star in the sky is this sort of egoist. The soul honors *itself* in its peers and the rights it yields to them; it never doubts that the exchange of honors and rights is the very *nature* of human intercourse, belonging to the natural order of things. The distinguished soul gives, as it takes, from the passionate and sensitive instinct for requital which lies at its very bottom. The concept of "mercy" has no meaning, no good odor, among equals; there may exist some sublime manner of taking gifts which drop like a gentle rain from above, and of sucking such droppings thirstily, but the distinguished soul has no talent for this skill or posture. Its egoism hinders it; it doesn't like to look "up" anyway, but prefers to look ahead, horizontally and slowly, or to look down. *It knows that it is on a height.*

### 266.

"One can truly honor only those who do not *seek* themselves."—Goethe to *Rath* Schlosser.

### 267.

The Chinese have a proverb which the mothers teach even to their little children: *siao-sin,* "make thy heart *small.*" This is the essential basic inclination of late civilizations; I do not doubt that an ancient Greek would first find out the self-belittlement among us Europeans of today. In this alone we should run "counter to his taste."—

### 268.

What, ultimately, is commonness?—Words are sound-symbols for concepts; concepts, however, are more or less definite image-symbols for frequently returning and concurring sensations, for sensation-groups. To use the same words is not a sufficient guarantee of understanding; one must use the same words for the same genus of inward experience; ultimately one must have one's experiences in *common*. That is why the people of one nation understand each other better than members of several nations even when they share a language; or rather, when people have lived with each other for a long time under similar conditions (of climate, soil, danger, needs, work), then there *arises* something from them that can "come to an understanding," i.e. a nation. A similar number of frequently returning experiences has gained the upper hand in everyone's psyche over those that occur more rarely; regarding them one comes to a more and more rapid understanding (the history of a language is the history of an abbreviation process); upon this rapid understanding one feels more and more closely allied. The greater the danger, the greater the need to agree quickly and easily on everything necessary: not to misunderstand one another in time of danger is what men cannot dispense with in their intercourse. It is a test that each friendship and each love-affair also undergoes. Nothing of this sort can endure as soon as the parties find out that one of the two using the same words feels, means, wishes, fears different things with them. (Fear of "eternal misunderstanding" is the well-meaning genius which often keeps persons of different sex from the over-eager attachments to which their senses and their hearts prompt them—*not* some Schopenhauerian "genius of the species"!) Which groups of sensations within a given psyche awaken most quickly, which ones come to expression, come to command—this is what decides the total order of its value, this is what in the end decides its table of goods. The value-estimates of a human being reveal something of the *structure* of his psyche, something of the way in which the psyche sees its basic conditions for life, its essential needs. Assuming now that need has always brought only those people together who could express similar needs and similar experiences with similar symbols, then we shall find, all things considered, that easy *communicability* of need, which means ultimately the experiencing of merely average and *common* experiences, must have been the most powerful of all the forces that have ever ruled mankind. The more alike and the more ordinary people were, and always are, at an advantage; the more select, subtle, and strange, those who are harder to understand, may easily remain alone; due to their solitary position they easily meet with accidents, and seldom propagate themselves. One must call upon enormous oppositional powers in order to contend against this natural, all-too natural *progressus in simile,* the continuous progress of man toward similarity, ordinariness, the average, the herd-like, the *common!*

### 269.

The more a psychologist—a born, irrepressible psychologist and soul-diviner—turns his attention to the more select cases and human beings, the greater becomes the danger that he will choke on compassion. He *needs* hardness and gay serenity more than other men. For the perishableness, the destructability, of superior human beings, of the rarer psychic types, is the rule: it is horrifying to have such a rule always before one's eyes. The psychologist who, at first once and then almost always and throughout history, discovers this destructability, the whole inner incurability[2] of the superior man, his everlasting "too late" in every sense, suffers a complex martyrdom which some day may cause him to turn against his own fate and attempt to destroy himself—to "perish." In almost every psychologist one will find a revealing inclination toward and pleasure in dealing with everyday, well-ordered human beings. What he reveals with this is that he always needs healing himself, that he needs a kind of escape and forgetting, away from the burdens that his insights and incisions, his "trade," have placed on his conscience. He is characterized by a fear of his own memory. He easily becomes silent when he hears the judgment of others; with an unmoved face he listens to them honoring, admiring, loving, and transfiguring something that he has *seen*—or else he hides even his silence by expressly agreeing with some foreground-opinion. Perhaps the paradox of his position goes so far toward the gruesome, that the masses, the educated people, the enthusiasts, learn their great reverence just where he has learned his great compassion plus his great contempt—the reverence for "great men," for the rare creatures for whose sake one blesses and honors one's fatherland, the earth, all human dignity, oneself; toward whom one guides and educates the youth. . . . And who knows whether the same thing did not happen in all the great cases thus far: the masses adored a god, and the "god" was only a poor sacrificial animal. Success has always been the worst of liars and even "works" are a form of success; the great statesman, the conqueror, the

---

[2] Nietzsche uses the word *Heillosigkeit* (from German *heilen,* heal) which suggests not only incurable (English "heal") but also lack of salvation (*Heil*-salvation; compare English "holy") and lack of wholeness (*heil*—English whole, hale). *Translator.*

discoverer are all disguised by their own creations to the point of unrecognizability; the "work" of the artist, the philosopher, really invents him who created it—who is supposed to have created it; the "great men" as they are honored are small poor fictions after the fact; in the world of historical values it is counterfeiting that rules. These great poets, for example, these Byrons, Mussets, Poes, Leopardis, Kleists, Gogols (I don't dare mention the greater names but I mean them)—such as they are and perhaps have to be, are men of the moment, enthusiastic, sensual, child-brained, equally irresponsible and precipitous in suspiciousness and confidence, the owners of souls that usually contain some kind of a fissure, often avenging in their works an inner defilement, often seeking release from an all too faithful memory, often lost in the swamps and almost in love with the swamps until they become like will-o'-the-wisps and can *pretend* to be stars—the people then call them idealists—often struggling with a long-lasting nausea, with an oft-returning ghost of unbelief that makes them cold and forces them to pant after "glory" and to eat "faith in themselves (and as such)" out of the hands of ecstatic flatterers—what a torture are these great artists and superior men in general for one who has found them out! It is so easy to understand how they receive those outbreaks of boundless and utterly devoted *compassion* from women—women being clairvoyant in the world of suffering and unfortunately possessed of a mania for helping and saving that which is far beyond their actual power to help and save. The masses, particularly the masses who honor and respect the artist, do not understand this phenomenon and overwhelm it with inquisitive and self-complaisant interpreta-

tions. The compassion of women is regularly deceived in its powers; they would like to believe that
love can do anything—it is their characteristic *superstition*. Alas, whoever knows the human heart
guesses how poor, helpless, pretentious, and blunder-
ing even the best and deepest love is—it destroys
more easily than it saves! It is possible that beneath
the holy fable and disguise of the life of Jesus there
is hidden one of the most painful instances of the
martyrdom that comes from *knowing about love:*
the martyrdom of the most innocent and greedy heart
that never ever got enough of human love, the heart
that *demanded* nothing other than love, than being
loved; who turned hardness, insanity, and frightful
explosions against all who denied their love; the history of a poor unsated and insatiable creature of love
who had to invent hell in order to send those who
didn't *want* to love him there—who finally, after he
had become knowing in human love, had to invent
a God who is entirely love, entirely *able* to love, who
takes pity on human love because it is so wretched,
so unknowing! Whoever feels this way, whoever
*knows* love in this fashion—*seeks* death. But why
ponder such painful matters? Assuming that one
does not have to. . . .

### 270.

The spiritual arrogance and nausea of every man
who has suffered deeply *(how* deeply men can suffer
almost determines the order of rank)—the gruesome certainty, which thoroughly imbues and colors
him, that by virtue of his suffering he *knows more*
than the shrewdest and wisest can know, that he has
been familiar with, and at home in, many distant,
dreadful words of which *"you* know nothing"—this

spiritual arrogance of the sufferer, this pride in being of the elite of insight, one of the initiate, one of the almost sacrificed, needs all forms of disguise in order to protect itself from contact with importunate and compassionate hands, and in general from everything that is not its equal in suffering. Deep suffering makes one distinguished; it draws distinctions. One of the most subtle forms of disguise is Epicureanism, along with a certain ostentatious courageousness of taste, which takes suffering lightly and takes a defensive stand against everything sad and profound. There are "serene men," who make use of serenity because they are misunderstood on account of it—they *want* to be misunderstood. There are "scientific men," who make use of science because science appears serene and because the scientific mind leads one to the conclusion that the scientist is concerned with the surface of things— such men *want* to lead us to a false conclusion. There are free brash spirits which would like to conceal and deny that they are broken, proud, incurable hearts (the cynicism of Hamlet—the case of Galiani); and occasionally it is folly itself that is the mask for an unhappy, all-too-knowing knowledge. From which it follows that it behooves a more subtle humaneness to have reverence "for the mask" and not to practice psychology and curiosity in the wrong place.

## 271.

What separates two human beings most deeply is their differing sense for degrees of cleanliness. What is the use of decency and mutual usefulness, what is the use of all good will toward one another, if in the end they cannot "stand each other's smell!" The highest instinct for cleanliness places the one who has it into the strangest, most dangerous solitude, as though he were a saint. For this *is* saintliness: the highest spiritualization of the above-named instinct. Some sort of knowledge of an indescribable wealth of the joys of bathing, some sort of ardor and thirst that constantly drives the soul out of the night into the morning and out of the gloom, the "gloominess" into the light, the glowing, the deep, the delicate. Such an inclination *separates* as much as it characterizes—it is a distinguished and distinguishing trait. The saint's compassion is compassion with the *filth* of the human, all too human. And there are degrees and heights where compassion itself is felt to be defilement, filth. . . .

### 272.

Signs of distinction: never to think of lowering our duties to be duties for everyman; not to yield, not to want to share, one's own responsibility; to count one's privileges and one's exercise of them among one's *duties*.

### 273.

A man who strives for great things regards everyone whom he meets on his way as either a means or a delay or an obstacle—or as a temporary bed to rest on. The highly developed *goodness* toward his fellowmen which is characteristic of him is not possible until he has reached his height and dominion. His impatience and his consciousness that he is meanwhile sentenced to be a character in a comedy (for even war is a comedy and hides something, just as every means hides its ends) spoil all his relations with other people; this type of man knows solitude and its worst poisons.

## 274.

*The Problem of Those Who Wait:* Lucky accidents and all sorts of incalculable things are necessary for a superior man in whom the solution of a problem is dormant to reach his action at the proper time—for his action to "break out," one might say. On the average it does *not* happen; in all corners of the earth there are human beings sitting and waiting, hardly knowing to what extent they are waiting and even less aware that they are waiting in vain. Occasionally the call to awakening, the accident that "permits" action comes too late—when their best youth and power to act has been used up by sitting; how many have found to their horror when they "jumped up" that their limbs were asleep, their spirits too heavy! "Too late," they tell themselves, having lost faith in themselves and being now forever useless. It is not possible in the realm of genius that some "Raphael without hands" [3] (taking the expression in its widest sense) is perhaps the rule rather than the exception? Perhaps genius is not so very rare at all; but rather the five hundred *hands* that it needs to tyrannize over the *kairos*, the "right moment," to seize chance by its forelock!

## 275.

Whoever does not *want* to see what is high in a man looks all the more sharply at what is low, and in the foreground. Thus he gives himself away.

[3] The implication is similar to that of Gray's "some mute inglorious Milton." *Translator.*

### 276.

The lower and coarser soul is better off in cases of any sort of injury and loss than the more distinguished one. The danger of the latter must be greater. The probability that it meets with an accident and perishes is, in fact, enormous, because of the complexity of the conditions necessary to its life. In a lizard a finger that has been lost will grow again; not so in a man.

### 277.

Too bad! Once more the same old story! When we have finished building our house we realize that we have inadvertently learned something which we should have known before we ever started to build. This everlasting baleful "too late!"—The melancholy of all that is *finished!* . . .

### 278.

Wanderer, who are you? I see you going your way, without scorn, without love, with unfathomable eyes, damp and sad like a plummet which has returned to the light from every depth without finding satisfaction. What was it seeking down below? I see your breast which does not heave, your lips that hide their nausea, your hands which are slow to touch anything—who are you? What were you doing? Come rest here; this place is hospitable for everyman; regain your strength! Whoever you may be, what would you like? What will serve to refresh you? Just name it: I offer you all that I have. "To refresh myself? To refresh myself? Oh you inquisitive man, what are you saying? But give me . . .

please give me. . . ." What? What? Tell me! "Another mask! A second mask!"—

### 279.

Men of profound sadness give themselves away when they are happy. They have a way of seizing happiness as though they wanted to crush it and choke it—out of jealousy. Ah, they know only too well that it will run away from them!

### 280.

"Bad! Bad! Look—isn't he going backward?" Yes, but you misunderstand him if you complain of it. He is going backward like someone who is about to take a great leap.—

### 281.

"Will people believe me?—But I demand that they believe me: I myself have never thought well of myself and about myself; I have thought of myself only in very rare cases; only when forced; always ready to digress from 'myself,' always without faith in the result—thanks to an irresistible distrust against the very possibility of self-recognition. it has led me so far as to sense a contradiction in terms in even the concept 'immediate self-knowledge' that the theoreticians permit themselves. This whole fact is almost the surest thing I know about myself. There must be an unwillingness in me to *believe* any definite thing about myself. Is there a riddle in that? Probably, but fortunately not one which I have to solve. Perhaps it reveals the species to which I belong—but not to me; and I like it that way.—"

### 282.

"But what has crossed your path?" "I don't know," he said hesitantly. "Perhaps the Harpies flew over my table."—It occasionally happens nowadays that a mild, moderate, reserved man suddenly flies into a rage; he smashes the plates, overturns the table, screams, raves, insults everybody—and finally withdraws, ashamed, furious with himself. Where is he going? What for? To starve in solitude? To choke on his memory? Whoever has the appetites of a superior discriminating soul but only rarely finds his table set and his meal prepared runs a great danger at all times. But today the danger is extraordinary. Flung into a noisy plebeian epoch, unable to eat from its dishes, he can easily perish of hunger and thirst or, in case he finally "takes a bite," of sudden nausea. All of us have probably at some time sat at tables where we did not belong, and those of us who are most intelligent, most difficult to nourish, know that dangerous dyspepsia which arises out of our sudden insight into and disappointment with the food and the others sitting at a table— the *after-dinner nausea*.

### 283.

There is a subtle and at the same time distinguished self-control in praising—if one wants to praise at all—only where one does not agree. Otherwise one would be praising oneself, which is not in good taste. It is a self-control, to be sure, which offers an excellent opportunity and provocation to be constantly *misunderstood*. To be able to afford this genuine luxury of taste and morality, one cannot live among idiots of the intellect; rather one must live among people whose misunderstandings and blunders afford delight in their very subtlety, or else one pays far too heavily for this pleasure! "He praises me, *hence* acknowledges that I am right."—This asinine inference ruins half our life for us anchorites, for it gives us asses for our neighbors and friends.

### 284.

To live in an immense and proud serenity: always "beyond"—to have and not to have one's passions, one's pro's and con's arbitrarily, to lower oneself to them, but only for hours at a time; to "sit down" on them, as though they were horses—often donkeys; for one must know how to utilize their stupidity as well as their fire. To preserve one's three hundred foregrounds; to retain one's dark glasses, for there are cases where no one should look us in the eye, much less into our motives. And to choose for one's company that roguish and joyful vice: courtesy. And to remain master of one's four virtues: courage, insight, fellow-feeling, and solitude. For solitude is a virtue in us, a sublime bent and bias for cleanliness that guesses how unavoidably unclean things get when human beings come in close contact, in "society." Any communion in any way, anywhere, at any time, makes for "commonness."

### 285.

The greatest events and thoughts (and the greatest thoughts are the greatest events) are comprehended most slowly. The generations which are their contemporaries do not experience, do not "live through" them—they live alongside them. What happens is similar to what happens in the stellar universe. The light of the remotest stars reaches men last; while

it has not yet reached them, they *deny* that there
are stars there. "How many centuries does it take
before a mind is fully comprehended?" That is also
a standard for creating an order of rank, a protocol,
such as is needed—for minds as well as for stars.—

### 286.

*"Hier ist die Aussicht frei, der Geist erhoben."* [4]
But there is also an opposite type of human being:
those who are also on a summit and have the prospect free—but are looking *down*.

### 287.

What is distinguished? What can the word "distinguished" still mean to us today? What reveals,
how does one recognize, the distinguished human
being beneath today's sky heavily overcast by the
beginnings of a plebeian rule that makes everything
opaque and leaden? It is not his actions by which
he can be proved: actions are always ambiguous,
always unfathomable; neither is it his "works."
Among artists and scholars there are many to be
found today who reveal through their works a drive,
a deep desire, for distinction. But precisely the need
*for* distinction is fundamentally different from the
needs of the distinguished soul. It is in fact the most
persuasive and dangerous mark of what they lack.
It is not works but "faith" that here decides, that
determines the order or rank—to reactivate an old
religious formula in a new and deeper sense. There
is some kind of basic certainty about itself which
a distinguished soul possesses, something which can-

[4] The prospect here is free; the mind looks upward.
(Goethe, *Faust*, Part II.)

not be sought nor found nor perhaps lost. *The distinguished soul has reverence for itself.*——

### 288.

There are people who have "intelligence" in an unavoidable way; they can turn and twist as they wish; they can cover their treacherous eyes with their hands (as though hands couldn't betray!), but in the end it appears again and again: they have something they wish to hide: intelligence. One of the subtlest means for deceiving others at least as long as possible, for successfully appearing dumber than one is (which, in ordinary life is as desirable as an umbrella) is called *enthusiasm,* including what goes with it—virtue, for example. For Galiani, who should know, said *vertu est enthousiasme.*

### 289.

If one listens to the footsteps of an anchorite, one can always hear something of an echo of desolation, something of the whisper and the fearful vigilance of solitude. In his strongest words, in his shriek even, there resounds a new, a more dangerous type of silence, of silent concealment. Whoever has sat alone with his soul year-in, year-out, day and night, in confidential discord and discourse, whoever became a cave-bear or a treasure seeker or a treasure guardian, a dragon, in his lair (which might be a labyrinth or a gold-mine)—in the end his very concepts will take on a unique twilight-color, an odor of depth as well as of mold, something incommunicative and repulsive that blows cold on anyone who passes by. The anchorite does not believe that any philosopher (assuming that all philosophers were once anchorites) ever expressed his essential and ultimate opinions in a book. On the contrary, one writes books in order to conceal what is concealed in one He will doubt, in fact, that a philosopher *can* ever have an "ultimate and essential" opinion. He will suspect behind each cave a deeper cave, a more extensive, more exotic, richer world beyond the surface, a bottomless abyss beyond every bottom," beneath every "foundation." Every philosophy is a foreground-philosophy: this is an anchorite's judgment. There is something arbitrary in the fact that the philosopher stopped *here,* that he looked back and looked around, that *here* he refrained from digging deeper, that he laid aside his spade. There is, in fact, something that arouses suspicion! Each philosophy also *conceals* a philosophy; each opinion is also a hiding place; each word is also a mask.

### 290.

Every deep thinker fears being understood more than he fears being misunderstood. His vanity may suffer from the latter, but his heart, his fellow-feeling suffers from the former. For it always says, "Why, oh why, do *you* want to have as hard a time as I do?"

### 291.

Man, a complex, lying, artificial, and inscrutable animal, weird-looking to the other animals not so much because of his power but rather because of his guile and shrewdness, has invented the clear conscience, so that he might have the sensation, for once, that his psyche is a *simple* thing. All of morality is a continuous courageous forgery, without which an enjoyment of the sight of man's soul would be impossible. From this point of view, the concept "art" may be much more comprehensive than one commonly believes.

## 292.

A philosopher: a human being who constantly experiences, sees, hears, suspects, hopes, and dreams the extraordinary; who is struck by his own thoughts as though they were external to him, as though they struck him from above and from below, who is struck by *his* type of events as though by lightning; who is himself perhaps a thunderstorm pregnant with new lightning flashes; a fateful man around whom there is a constant grumbling and rumbling, sudden illuminations of gaping abysses, and all sorts of uncanny mysteries. A philosopher: alas, a creature who often runs away from himself—but so inquisitive that he always "comes to" again, to himself.

## 293.

A man who says "I like this; I take it for my own; I will protect it and defend it against everyman," a man who can plead a cause, carry out a resolution, remain faithful to an idea, hold a woman, punish and lay low a transgressor; a man who has his anger and his sword, to whom the weak, the suffering, the oppressed, and the animals as well like to belong, and by nature do belong—in short a man who is a natural *master*—when *such* a man feels compassion, then such compassion is worth something! But of what use is the compassion of those who suffer? Or even worse, of those who *preach* compassion? Almost everywhere in Europe today there is a pathological sensibility and sensitivity for pain; also a repulsive excess of lamentation, a weakness which would like to pretend with the help of religion and philosophical bric-a-brac that it is a superiority; there is a regular cult of suffering. The *unmanliness* of that which is called "compassion" in such circles of devotees is in my opinion only too obvious. One must resolutely and fundamentally taboo this type of bad taste; for protection against it, I wish one might wear the good amulet *"gai saber"* around one's heart and neck (*Frohliche Wissenschaft* —to make it plainer to the Germans)![5]

### 294.

*The Olympian Vice.* In spite of that philosopher (Hobbes) who, as a genuine Englishman, sought to ruin the reputation of laughter, claiming that it is a terrible infirmity of human nature which every rational mind should seek to overcome, I should permit myself an ordering of the ranks of philosophers according to the quality of their laughter—all the way up to those who are capable of *golden* laughter. And if the gods, too, philosophize (a conclusion to which I have often been driven), I do not doubt that they also know how to laugh in a superhuman and original fashion—and at the expense of all serious things! Gods like to mock; it seems that they cannot refrain from laughter even in the presence of holy acts.

### 295.

*Genius of the hearts*: as it is possessed by that great Hidden One, the Tempter-God and born Rat-Catcher of the Conscience, whose voice can climb into the underworld of any psyche, who never speaks a word or looks a look in which there is not some hind-sight, some complexity of allure, whose crafts-

[5] See section 260, Note 1.

manship includes knowing how to be an illusion—
not an illusion of what he is, but of what constitutes
one more compulsion upon his followers to follow
him ever more intimately and thoroughly—*genius
of the heart* which renders dumb all that is loud and
complaisant, teaching it how to listen, which smooths
rough souls and creates a taste in them for a new
desire: to lie still like a mirror so that the deep
sky might be reflected in them—*genius of the heart*
which teaches the bungling and precipitous hand
to hesitate and handle things delicately, which
guesses the hidden and forgotten treasure, the drop
of goodness and sweet intelligence beneath layers
of murky, thick ice; which is a divining rod for
every speck of gold that lies buried in its dungeon
of deep muck and sand—*genius of the heart,* upon
whose touch everyone departs richer, not full of
grace, not surprised, not enriched and oppressed as
though by strange goods, but richer in himself, newer
than before, cracked wide open, blown upon and
drawn out by a spring wind, more uncertain now
perhaps, more delicate, fragile, and broken, but
full of hopes that have no names as yet, full of
new will and flow, full of new ill will and counter-
flow—but what am I doing, my friends? Of whom
am I speaking? Did I forget myself so far as not
to tell you his name? Unless you yourselves have
guessed who this questionable spirit and God is;
who it is that demands such praise! For, as happens
to everyone who from his early years has been a
wanderer and an exile, many a strange and precarious spirit has run across my path. Foremost of all
of them, and again and again, the one I was telling
you about, no less a one that the God *Dionysos,*
that great Ambivalent One and Tempter-God, the

one to whom I once, as you know, in all secrecy
and all reverence, sacrificed my first-born[6] (having
been the last, it seems to me, to sacrifice anything
to him, for I found no one who understood what I
was doing at that time). Meanwhile I learned much,
all too much, about this God's philosophy by word
of mouth, as I have said—I, the last disciple and
initiate of the God Dionysos. It is really time, therefore, to give you, my friends, a small taste of this
philosophy, insofar as I am permitted. *Sotto voce*,
as is proper, for it is a matter of many things that
are mysterious, new, exotic, strange, uncanny. Even
that Dionysos is a philosopher and hence that gods
philosophize seems to me a piece of precarious news,
designed to create suspicion among philosophers.
Among you, my friends, it is probably safer to tell
it—unless it is told too late or at the wrong time—
for you no longer like to believe in God or any gods
nowadays, as you tell me. Furthermore, I may have
to be more frank in my tale than the stern habits
of your ears will like. In any event, the God in
question always went further, a great deal further,
when *he* held such discourses; he was always many
steps ahead of me. . . . If it were allowed, I should
accord him, as is the human custom, many beautiful
solemn titles of pomp and virtue, much extolling of
his explorer's and discoverer's courage, of his daring
candor, his truthfulness, his love for wisdom. But a
God such as he does not know what to do with such
respectable clap-trap and pomp. "Keep it," he would
say, "keep it for yourself and whoever is like you,
whoever else needs such stuff! I have no reason to
cover my nakedness!" One may easily guess that this

---

[6] Nietzsche alludes to his first work, *Die Geburt der
Tragödie*, Tr.

type of divinity and philosopher lacks modesty. Once, for example, he said "I love mankind under certain conditions" (alluding to Ariadne who was there at the time), "man seems to me to be a pleasant, courageous, inventive animal who has not his likes on earth; he can find his way around any labyrinth. I wish him well; I often contemplate how I might advance him, how I might make him stronger, more evil, and deeper than he is." "Stronger, more evil, and deeper?" I asked, shocked. "Yes," he said once more, "stronger, more evil, deeper, and also—more beautiful"—and saying this he smiled his halcyon smile, this Tempter-God, as though he had delivered himself of an enchanting courtesy. One sees at once that t is not only modesty which this divinity lacks. . . . here are good reasons, in fact, for supposing that a the gods could learn from us men in several respects. We men are more—humane. . . .

### 296.

Alas, what are you in the end, my written and painted thoughts? Not long ago you were so brightly colored, so young and wicked, so full of thorns and secret spices that you made me sneeze and laugh— and now? You have taken off your newness; some of you, I fear, are ready to turn into truths, so immortal do you already look, so heart-breakingly decent, so boring And was it ever otherwise? What sort of thing do we copy down, we mandarins with our Chinese brushes, we immortalizers of the things that *can* be written? What are we able to copy down? Only, alas, what is about to fade and lose its fragrance! Only departing and exhausted thunderstorms, alas, and belated yellow feelings! Only birds, alas, who flew till they were weary and lost their way, who can be caught in the hand—in *our* hand! We immortalize what has not long to live, what can no longer soar—tired and hollow things! It is only your afternoon, you my written and painted thoughts, for which I have the right colors—perhaps many colors, many bright-colored tendernesses, fifty yellows and browns and greens and reds. But no one could guess from these how you looked during your morning, you flashing sparks and miracles of my solitude—you old beloved *wicked* thoughts of mine!

# POSTLUDE

## FROM THE SUMMITS

Oh solemn time! Oh zenith of life's day!
Oh summer's thronging!
Oh restless joy in looking, standing, longing
For friends to come; prepared by night and day—
The time has come! Friends, do not stay away!

Grey glaciers rosy-wreathed themselves for you.
Toward you unheeding
Leaps the brook. Yearning, seething,
The winds and clouds push high into the blue
In distant auspicy to look for you.

On highest peaks for you my table's spread:
What rookery
Perches so steeply between pit and galaxy?
Whose empire's boundaries lie so far ahead?
Who'll eat my honey to be sweetly fed?

You've come, my friends!—Alas you say I'm not
Whom you foresaw?
You hesitate? I'd rather you found flaw!
No longer I? Some other face, hands, trot?
And what I am—for you I'm simply not?

A wrestler whose self-victory is his self-disgrace?
You say I've changed,
Become a stranger, from myself estranged?
Too often labored my own strength to displace,
Wounded and checked by winning my own race?

I searched where only sharp winds play?
I learned to wander
Where no one goes, in icy barrens yonder?
Forgot both man and God, forgot to curse, to pray,
Became the ghost that walks the glaciers grey?

237

My dear old friends, fear clutches at your throat,
Love and pale anguish;
Go back in peace, here you would only languish.
Here between ice and rock, rough and remote,
One must be both the hunter and the goat.

With tight-strung bow a wickd hunter I became—
Its quivering tension
Bespeaks the hunter's powerful dimension—
Beware and flee: this arrow's dangerous aim
Is like none other: this is not a game!

You turn away? Heart, you have borne your pain;
Strong in hoping,
For *new* friends hold your gates now open!
Let go the others, drop memory's refrain!
Once you were young, now be—young again!

What once we shared, our mutual hopes' tie—
There's no evading
Our fate—love's cipher now is fading.
It is a parchment that the hand is shy
Of touching: crumbled, scorched, and dry.

No longer friends—what name shall I invent?
Friends apparition—
It begs at heart and window for admission;
A sad "We *were* the ones" is its lament:
Oh withered words that once were redolent!

Oh youthful hope for my own kind of loyalty!
The vain elation
That I had loyal-changing friends was my imagination.
The spell of getting old has made them flee:
Only a man who changes can be true to me.

Oh second youth! Oh zenith of life's day!
Oh summer's thronging!
Oh restless joy in looking, standing, longing
For friends to come; prepared by night by day—
The time has come! *New friends,* do not stay away!

This song is sung: longing's sweet cry grew
And died. It heeded
The magic of the friend who came when needed,
The noon-hour friend—no, do not ask me who—
It was at noon when One turned into Two.

At last our common victory's in sight,
The feast I seek—
Friend *Zarathustra* came, the guest unique,
Now the world laughs down terror's blight,
The wedding day is here for dark and light. . . .

# Gateway Titles

GENTZ, FRIEDRICH, & POSSONY, *Three Revolutions*

HANNA, THOMAS, *The Thought and Art of Albert Camus*

HARVEY, WILLIAM, *On the Motion of the Heart and Blood*

HEIDEGGER, MARTIN, *Existence and Being*

HITTI, PHILIP K., *The Arabs—A Short History*

HOBBES, THOMAS, *Leviathan I*

HOFFMAN, FREDERICK J., *Modern Novel in America*

HUME, DAVID, *Enquiry Concerning Human Understanding; Abstract of A Treatise on Human Nature*

JASPERS, KARL, *Nietzsche and Christianity*

JOHNSON, HOWARD A. AND NIELS THULSTRUP, *A Kierkegaard Critique*

JOHNSON, SAMUEL, *Lives of the English Poets*

JUENGER, F. G., *The Failure of Technology*

KIRK, RUSSELL, *The Conservative Mind*

KLAASEN, ADRIAN, *The Invisible Hand*

LEONHARD, WOLFGANG, *Child of the Revolution*

LEWIS, WYNDHAM, *Self Condemned*

LOCKE, JOHN, *Essay Concerning Human Understanding* (Abridged)

LOCKE, JOHN, *Of Civil Government*

LOCKE, JOHN, *On the Reasonableness of Christianity*

MACHIAVELLI, NICCOLO, *The Prince*

MAISTRE, JOSEPH de, *On God and Society*

MARCEL, GABRIEL, *Man Against Mass Society*

MARCEL, GABRIEL, *Metaphysical Journal*

MARCEL, GABRIEL, *The Mystery of Being*, Vols. I & II

MARCUS AURELIUS, *Meditations* (with EPICTETUS, *Enchiridion*)

MARX, KARL, *Das Kapital* (Abridged)

MARX, KARL, *Communist Manifesto*

MAYER, PETER, ed., *The Pacifist Conscience*

MILL, JOHN STUART, *Considerations on Representative Government*